FLAGS OF CANADA

FLAGS OF CANADA

The Right Honourable
Stephen J. Harper

TORONTO, 2025

Sutherland House
416 Moore Ave., Suite 304
Toronto, ON M4G 1C9

First edition, February 2025

If you are interested in inviting one of our authors to a live event or media appearance, please contact sranasinghe@sutherlandhousebooks.com and visit our website at sutherlandhousebooks.com for more information.

We acknowledge the support of the Government of Canada.

Manufactured in Canada
Cover designed by Leah Ciani, Shalomi Ranasinghe, and Jordan Lunn
Illustrations by Greg Stoicoiu
Book composed by Karl Hunt

Library and Archives Canada Cataloguing in Publication
Title: Flags of Canada / the Right Honourable Stephen J. Harper.
Names: Harper, Stephen, 1959- author
Description: Includes bibliographical references.
Identifiers: Canadiana (print) 20240538110 | Canadiana (ebook) 20240538161 | ISBN 9781998365494 (hardcover) | ISBN 9781998365500 (EPUB)
Subjects: LCSH: Flags—Canada—History. | LCSH: Canada—History.
Classification: LCC CR115.C3 H37 2025 | DDC 929.9/20971—dc23

ISBN 978-1-998365-49-4
eBook 978-1-998365-50-0

Contents

This book about the past is dedicated to my future – Ben and Rachel.

Introduction

MY EARLIEST POLITICAL memory is the flag debate of 1964–1965. I was a kindergarten pupil when the new national flag was hoisted above Toronto's Northlea[1] Elementary School for the first time. It is a day I remember vividly.

As a five-year-old, I had been intrigued by the different designs that had been proposed for the new flag. I naively decided to ask family, friends, and neighbours which option they preferred. Perhaps I should have known better. The responses I received in the normally hospitable surroundings of Leaside were quiet and sullen. People did talk to me, but it became apparent they were not talking to one another. Differences ran deep.

What I learned was that the preference for one flag option over another was seldom about the design. To use terms I discovered when I was much older, it was really about identity, history, and the collective narratives in which one believed.

In any case, it was the designs that drew my attention as a young boy. It was a great time to become interested in flags. Not only did Canada have its new flag, but the provinces were in the process of adopting their own flags, and so were many municipalities. The various national and provincial centennials soon produced many more. I accumulated an impressive little collection of "hand waver" versions of those flags.

That, in turn, sparked my interest in Canadian history, for good flags are permeated with historical symbolism. My interest in Canadian history took me back to the beginning. That beginning, I discovered, was well before the events whose centennial we would celebrate in 1967.

Indigenous peoples long had their own marks of nationhood. Most Canadian state symbols originated with the European imperial powers who laid the foundations of our institutions. By far, the most important were the French and British, with John Cabot establishing the first British claims in 1497 and Jacques Cartier doing the same for the French in 1534.

The real point of departure rests with Samuel de Champlain and the founding of Quebec, Canada's first capital, in 1608. This book thus begins with the flags of New France and their legacy.

By 1763, the French regime had been entirely displaced by the British, under whom the eventual boundaries of the state began to take shape. The second section thus examines the key flags of British North America and their legacy.

While the transition from British rule to Canadian independence was gradual, our institutions of state were created by Confederation in 1867. It is from there that I will examine the emergence of a distinctive flag of Canada in the final section.

The purpose of this book, first and foremost, is to illustrate the key flags of Canadian history, from the continental banners of New France and British North America to the debates over a national flag for Canada. My friend Greg Stoicoiu has produced vivid images of these banners (I did not want to "borrow" images from the internet, so I commissioned Greg, an artist who is legally blind, to do this work). Our hope is that these renderings will visually interest the reader, as they once did for this young boy in Leaside, and spark interest in the history and meaning of these colourful symbols.

The commentary that accompanies these depictions is designed to inform the reader about the story behind these flags. I do express the occasional opinion, particularly in the third section. Still, my purpose is not to push anyone into embracing a particular narrative around a flag design or about the system it represents.

It is my view that some otherwise fine histories of Canadian flags have been marred by narrative-centric tales. These have portrayed the advocates of certain designs as heroes, while those preferring other designs come across as villains or deluded naysayers. These caricatures are a disservice to history. They obscure the nuances and complexities of historical truth.

Of course, readers are free to embrace these, or any other narratives. My only hope is that, as they reach their conclusions, they base them on facts. A worthy opinion should have the facts as a minimum benchmark.

1

The Flags of New France and Their Legacy

CHAMPLAIN'S TINY SETTLEMENT at Quebec would become the political centre of New France, the immense viceroyalty of the Kingdom of France in the New World (see Figure 1). At its heart was the region along the St. Lawrence River called Canada. That term gradually took on a wider meaning, encompassing much of our present-day country. New France as a whole was much larger than Canada today: it included the Ohio, Missouri, and Mississippi valleys, all the way to the Gulf of Mexico.

New France, however, was a paper giant. Even in its St. Lawrence heartland, it was sparsely populated and the French claims were contested by the British from the outset. In retrospect, with the British population in North America outnumbering the French by over twenty to one, New France was doomed. France conceded its territory by treaty in 1763. Today the small islands of St. Pierre and Miquelon off the coast of Newfoundland are the only remnants of France's North American empire.

But those islands are not New France's only legacy. While the British took over the government in Quebec, the Francophone population remained largely intact. In two subsequent conflicts, they helped sustain British rule. And, so, the continental state they founded, while it changed dramatically, would also endure.

This heritage manifests itself in various national and regional flags and symbols, a sampling of which is discussed in the following section.

The Flag of the Kingdom of France

What was the national flag of France during the period of New France's existence? The answer to this question is far from straightforward, although our country does have an official position on the issue. Canada's coat of arms since 1921 has sported a unicorn supporter. The mythical creature holds the flag—the *Bannière de France* (see Figure 2)—that we have designated as France's during the period of its rule over Canada.

A couple of broad observations on the style of this flag are in order. The *Bannière de France* is here shown as square and flying horizontally, but this was not always the case. Over the centuries, the conventional shape of flags has evolved significantly.

In antiquity, flags were typically vertical, especially Roman and religious banners. In the Middle Ages, long, swallow-tailed pennants became common. These tended to become shorter, often with multiple points. Square flags seem to have been in vogue during the early colonial period (roughly the 1500s and 1600s). Later and gradually, they take on longer, rectangular shapes. Today, a flag is often illustrated as 2:1 (width to height), even when those are not its official proportions.

The language of heraldry is blazon, a specialized jargon rooted in Norman English. It does not always specify a flag's shape, and it rarely identifies the exact tone of its colour. The shades can and do evolve. For instance, blue flags have tended to darken in shade over the centuries. As for the *Bannière de France*, it was usually the royal blue shown in Canada's coat of arms, but versions in a pale greenish blue, sky blue, dark blue, and violet are known to have existed.[2]

The banner includes fleurs-de-lis, ancient symbols of uncertain origin, which also have changed considerably over the ages. Again, the precise styles were not often specified in heraldic descriptions, so we cannot be sure what designs were officially or even typically used. Before modern manufacturing, flags were individually made, and there are precious few extant banners from the period in which New France existed.

A much larger issue than the specifics of the *Bannière de France* is whether it was really the national flag of France. The claim is highly contentious. Indeed, it is almost certainly false. Royal France did not have a "national flag" as we understand the term today.[3] After all, the absolutist kingdom was the extension of its ruler, not the expression of a nation. Its flags were the king's own or attached to the offices and the institutions he created.

Truth be told, the notion of a single national flag—one for a wide range of state, civil, and military functions on both land and sea—is relatively modern. Canada has one today, but the Kingdom of France was marked by a great diversity of flags. A 1661 ordinance of Louis XIV listed some sixty-eight designs authorized for various institutions and functions. Moreover, these changed frequently over the centuries, although there were commonalities, with blue, white, and red generally considered royal colours[4] and the gold fleurs-de-lis as the most frequent royal symbol.

Yet the *Bannière de France* had, since the later Middle Ages, taken on some of the broader usage typical of a national flag. It was originally the king's flag and had been derived from the royal shield. Initially, it displayed a large, undefined quantity of fleurs-de-lis, a style described as *France ancien*. By the fourteenth century, the number of fleurs-de-lis had been reduced to three—called *France moderne*—symbolizing the Holy Trinity.[5]

The *Bannière de France* is believed to have flown on at least three occasions in the early days of New France. It is shown in a drawing of the ill-fated Fort Caroline (in today's Florida) in 1564. It is referenced in 1604 records from St. Croix in Acadia. It would also appear to be depicted in a two-tailed form in Champlain's sketch of Quebec in 1610.[6] Nevertheless, from the early seventeenth century, this flag was seen less frequently.[7]

Was the *Bannière de France* replaced by a similar general-use flag? The answer is yes, but with one not as readily identifiable with the kingdom as France.[8] In fact, the French, beginning with Jacques Cartier, tended to mark their sovereignty in North America with the royal shield rather than a flag.

This suggests that the *Bannière de France* is as reasonable a proxy for the national flag of royal France as any.[9]

One last note is in order. The *Bannière de France* has not entirely vanished. It continues to be used as the unofficial banner of Île-de-France, the administrative region around Paris.

French Ensigns

The term "ensign" (French *Pavillon*) often refers to the principal flag used on ships. Ensigns were very influential in Canadian colonial history. Carried on boats from the homeland, they were among the most frequently seen flags on this side of the Atlantic, thereby engendering a strong sense of identity.

The French *Pavillon rouge* (see Figure 3) came into use in the fifteenth century. Initially a battle flag, it also served as a general ensign. Its design stemmed from its origins in the Hundred Years' War, being the colours of the enemy English flag in reverse. The *Pavillon rouge* was so widely employed that, for a time, it might have become an unofficial national flag.[10] But it had disadvantages, including its close resemblance to the flags of Denmark and Switzerland.

The *Pavillon rouge* did not disappear. Rather, it morphed into a wide range of French flags based on the white cross.[11] These had varying colour patterns in the quadrants, with fleurs-de-lis or other symbols sometimes added. Most of the regiments that served in New France had flags of this basic design.[12]

We do not know if the *Pavillon rouge* ever appeared in Canada. Cartier may have sailed under it. However, he more likely used its successor for the merchant marine, the *Pavillon bleu* (see Figure 4). Champlain certainly did.[13]

The *Pavillon bleu* would have appeared routinely on commercial ships in New France. This pattern is sometimes known as the St. Michael's Cross, the archangel being a patron saint of France. The royal shield was later added to the centre of this ensign and, eventually, the crown and collars of the royal arms were inserted as well. However, there is no evidence that these enhanced versions were ever used in New France.[14]

Instead, merchantmen began to prefer a different flag and, for them, a prohibited one, the *Pavillon blanc* (see Figure 5). This should not be confused with the flags of many regimental colonels, which consisted of a white cross with white quadrants. The *Pavillon blanc* was an undifferentiated white ensign with a different origin. That lineage is traced from the Middle Ages, including from the white banner used by Joan of Arc, which also sported gold fleurs-de-lis and religious symbols.

The *Pavillon blanc* was the French naval ensign. As such, it found its way to North America after New France became a royal colony in 1663. It appeared not only on royal vessels, but also over forts manned by the royal marines. Indeed, this flag was used in a range of circumstances in the later stages of the Kingdom of France. By the end of the *ancien régime* (or before the French Revolution), it had become the de facto national flag—the white representing the French monarchy's claim to be the pure and true defender of the Catholic faith.

French Colonial Flags

When I was a boy, the flag of New France was widely thought to have been white with gold fleurs-de-lis. Typically, a large number of fleurs-de-lis were shown, but, as with the *Bannière de France*, this could be reduced to three. For this reason, I shall call such a flag the *Bannière blanche* (see Figure 6).

Modern vexillologists (people who study flags) have disputed this view. Neither New France nor any part of it had an official flag. As for the *Bannière blanche*, no such flag appears to have ever had any legal status, and there is only a scant record of flags of that type in the New World.[15]

The truth is that we have very little documentary evidence regarding the flags that flew in New France. The few contemporary drawings of banners above buildings are shown in black and white and are generally imprecise.[16] Later, artistic depictions of flags almost invariably reflect the age in which they were painted, not the one they purport to represent.

What we do know is that the inhabitants of New France clearly identified white as their national colour.[17] It was reflected in the typically white (or off-white) uniforms of the French infantry. More pointedly, it was symbolized by the growing use of the *Pavillon blanc*.

The *Pavillon blanc* suffered from a serious drawback, however. While it could present a clear and striking image in high-quality cloth on the high seas or the battlefield, its plainness made it an ambiguous emblem. Its likeness to the age-old and universal flag of truce was an obvious problem. Frankly, unless one understood the national context, the *Pavillon blanc* contained no clear French symbolism.

This problem was solved, when necessary, by the inclusion of French symbols on the *Pavillon blanc*. These could be religious images or, indeed, gold fleurs-de-lis. For official purposes, the royal shield was added, sometimes with other elements of the royal arms. The use of this *Pavillon blanc aux armes* (see Figure 7) was documented on at least two occasions in New France.[18]

The *Pavillon blanc aux armes* was probably the closest thing to a flag of New France. Its use of the royal shield and the dominant white colour were the two clearest symbolic manifestations of French authority and identity in North America. It was paralleled in the adoption of Red Ensign designs by British colonists.[19] Both types of flags were based on the dominant maritime ensign, in the predominant national colour, and sported national symbolism.

This begs a question. What was the basis of the long-held view that the flag of New France was the *Bannière blanche*? It starts with the recognition that such flags existed as far back as Joan of Arc.[20] They were frequently depicted in paintings over the centuries. As for the New France claim, the earliest written example I have found is an 1855 speech by Pierre-Joseph-Olivier Chauveau, a future premier of Quebec.[21] It was evidently common knowledge then.

My own view is that the *Bannière blanche* was probably used in New France, just as it was in the mother country. The modern argument against this largely stems from the observation that no such flag had official standing. But that is a point in its favour. Under the *ancien régime*, one would have been very hesitant to fly a flag officially authorized for some other purpose. It is certainly conceivable that some in New France painted or stitched gold or yellow fleurs-de-lis on white cloth to make an unofficial patriotic flag, one clearly distinguishable from a flag of truce.

I concede that I may simply be reluctant to give up a belief adopted in childhood. Whether it was used or not, we shall see that the *Bannière blanche* has something of a legacy in North America.

The Flag of Quebec

The core of the viceroyalty of New France is now the heart of the province of Quebec, where the symbols of royal France endure. For example, Quebec's coat of arms today contains a trinity of gold fleurs-de-lis on blue, reminiscent of the *Bannière de France.* Nonetheless, the legacy of New France in the modern flag of Quebec was quite circuitous.

After the conquest of New France, French flags were quickly displaced by British ones, and it was some decades before unique local flags began to appear in Quebec (then Lower Canada). The first to gain traction was the *Tricolore canadien.* It consisted of horizontal stripes of green, white, and red, presumably representing the Irish, French, and British populations. That flag was tainted by its association with the failed rebellion against British colonial rule in 1837–1838. However, it is still employed in Quebec on occasion by ultra-nationalist groups, variants having popped up as recently as the Ottawa trucker protests of 2022.[22]

The next flag to attract a wide following was none other than the *Tricolore français,* the flag of republican France. This coincided with the growing closeness of British-French relations, particularly during the Crimean War and the visit of the frigate *La Capricieuse* to Quebec in 1855. The first French ship to arrive in Canada since the conquest, it was greeted by the sight of its national flag flying over Francophone and Anglophone homes alike.

By the close of the nineteenth century, Canadians were engaged in the country's first full-fledged flag debate. As Anglophones were in the process of elevating the status of the Union Jack nationally, Francophones began to entertain designs for their own unique banner. Among those were proposals for Canadianizing the *Tricolore français,* including by putting a maple leaf in the white panel. However, Francophone communities of the day, most especially their Catholic leaders, were deeply allergic to the secular ethos of republican France. They sought a flag rooted in their faith and history.

Despite its resemblance to the *Pavillon bleu*, Quebec's flag is not a direct descendant of the old French merchant ensign. That parenthood goes to the *Drapeau de Carillon* (see Figure 8). Today, residing in the *Musée de l'Amérique francophone* in Quebec City, it is the only fully surviving banner of the New France era. It is also the stuff of legend, quite literally.

Legend placed the flag, made around 1726, with the French-Canadian militia at the 1758 battle of Carillon. As it flew, the Virgin Mary was said to have appeared, her robes absorbing the British fire. The banner and the apparition led the French, outnumbered five to one, to their last great victory before the conquest in 1760.

The flag was later carried to Quebec with French General Louis-Joseph de Montcalm's retreating forces and hung in the church of the Récollets.

In 1796, it was fortuitously saved from a fire that destroyed the building. It then disappeared until being re-discovered in 1847 in a trunk belonging to the last surviving member of the Récollets order.

On the centenary of the famous battle, the nationalist poet Octave Crémazie composed a long ode. It immortalized the *Drapeau de Carillon* in the popular imagination. By that time, the banner was very old, and its rare public appearances provoked scenes of nationalist and religious fervour.[23]

The poem and its story were quintessential examples of the mythic French-Canadian nationalism of those times. It attributed the survival of the French-Canadian people, their language, and their culture, not to political acts and public policy, but to the strength and endurance of their Catholic faith. In fact, the famous flag was not a battle relic at all, but a religious banner, hung vertically, with the reverse side showing the Virgin Mary holding the baby Jesus.

In 1902, the Quebec parish priest Elphège Filiatrault proposed modifying the *Drapeau de Carillon*. His aim was to create a French-Canadian national flag, the *Carillon moderne* (see Figure 9). Father Filiatrault chose a sky-blue colour,[24] positioned the fleurs-de-lis to point to the middle, and gave them a more contemporary form. He also replaced the shield with a white cross to provide a more pious echo of ancestral France.

Father Filitrault's design was taken up by the Catholic establishment in 1903. Despite his objections, the hierarchy inserted the "Sacred Heart of Jesus," as urged by Pope Leo XIII, and surrounded it with a laurel of maple leaves. With the power of the church and the lay organizations behind it, the *Carillon Sacré-Coeur* (see Figure 10) gradually became the de facto flag of French-Canadians. It was officially assigned to the *Société Saint-Jean-Baptiste* by the Quebec Legislature in 1926.

In the late 1940s, the federal and provincial governments were in the midst of yet another flag debate. In Quebec, pressure mounted for adoption of a Carillon-style flag as the official provincial banner. Opinion was by then indifferent toward inclusion of the sacred heart.

The nationalist-conservative premier, Maurice Duplessis, was initially reluctant. He preferred a design based on the provincial shield. Such a flag was even used on one occasion in 1938.[25] However, in early 1948, Duplessis came around to the more popular option, with a twist. He removed the Sacred Heart and put the fleurs-de-lis upright in the centre of the quadrants. In so doing, he not only created a better-proportioned banner, but he also made the *Drapeau du Québec* (see Figure 11) his own. The *"Fleurdelisé"* would be an enduring legacy for Quebec's longest-serving premier.

The secular and republican sovereignists who waved Duplessis's flag in the decades following the Quiet Revolution seemed oblivious to its religious and royal character. To them, it said only "Quebec." This shows how a flag can become a symbol in its own right.

And quite a symbol it is. The *Fleurdelisé* displays all the characteristics that experts assign to outstanding flags. It uses just two basic colours that strongly contrast, with symbolism that is simple but meaningful and organized in a distinctive pattern.[26] This exceptionally elegant design has been rated as one of the best subnational flags in North America.[27]

Other French Legacy Flags

The symbols of the French Kingdom have atrophied in their homeland, certainly at the national level. However, they are common among the communities descended from New France, on the American as well as the Canadian side of the border. For example, the flags of Baton Rouge, Detroit, Mobile, and St. Louis are among the many that contain fleurs-de-lis. Various combinations of yellow, white, and blue are typically used.

Even today, when these or other locales depict the flag of New France, as some do, for example, on coats of arms, they invariably use the *Bannière blanche*. The *France ancien* style is usually chosen. One of the better-known examples is the "six flags of Texas," which refers to the six sovereign entities that have historically ruled there. This flag always represents the French period.

Still, no contemporary flag bears as striking a resemblance to the *Bannière blanche* (in its *France moderne* incarnation) as the *Drapeau de la Nouvelle-Orléans* (see Figure 12). The flag of New Orleans was not designed until 1918. That means it plausibly can be credited to the outdated theory of New France's flag.

It is harder to discount the homegrown *Drapeau de la Rivière-Rouge* (see Figure 13). This was the flag of Red River's rebellious provisional government of 1869–1870, led by Louis Riel and the Francophone Métis. To be clear, there was no single official version, and I have admittedly chosen the one closest to the *Bannière blanche*. That said, this version is typical. All the known examples were white with fleurs-de-lis, which were almost always yellow. The green shamrock, presumably representing the Anglophone Métis (at least the Catholic ones), was also standard. So, too, was the brown buffalo, a unifying local symbol adopted by the successor province of Manitoba.[28]

Another notable French legacy flag in the Americas is the *Drapeau aux serpents* (see Figure 14) of the Caribbean island of Martinique. Still an overseas territory of France, Martinique's "Snake Flag" bears an uncanny resemblance to Quebec's, and there is no doubt about its roots in the *Pavillon bleu*. While it was used as an unofficial flag for over 200 years, the Snake Flag has fallen into disrepute due to its historical association with the slave trade. Martinique adopted a temporary alternative in 2019 and a permanent replacement in 2023, both of which are local designs.

Some mention should be made of the French-Canadian flags of the various provinces and territories. Most of these are even more recent creations than the official provincial and territorial flags, having been adopted since 1975. They also generally employ the royal fleur-de-lis in some form. There is, however, one notable exception, the *Drapeau acadien* (see Figure 15).

The Acadian flag is based on the *Tricolore français*, with the addition of the *Stella Maris*—the star of the Virgin Mary and an Acadian national symbol. The banner became official in 1884, when the republican flag was at the height of its popularity among French-Canadians. The fact that the Francophones of the Maritimes had little cultural connection to the French Republic is irrelevant. Age alone has made this flag their distinctive emblem.

2

The Flags of British North America and Their Legacy

THE CONQUEST OF New France was essentially completed in 1760. Its last governor surrendered to the British at Montreal, burning all the French flags before he did so. That act prevented the enemy from taking regimental colours as trophies. But it also explains in part why no flags of New France remain—the famous *Drapeau de Carillon* being the major exception.

In any case, the British were present in the country long before the conquest. Newfoundland had its first English resident governor, John Guy, in 1610, over half a century before the French presence in *Terre Neuve*. Control of France's *Acadie*, or Britain's Nova Scotia, swung back and forth from the early 1600s. In what New France called the *Nord canadien*, the Hudson's Bay Company carved out the fur-trading empire of Rupert's Land from 1670 onward. After 1763, the fur trade would extend into the unknown lands of the North-Western Territory. Even the core of Canada itself—the British would call it Quebec—had been briefly occupied in the early part of the seventeenth century (see Figure 16).

The British possessions in what is now Canada are literally only half the story. The conquest combined the northern and formerly French territories with the thirteen British colonies on the Atlantic seaboard and previously Spanish Florida. British America thus covered the entire eastern half of the continent. However, it was to be a brief interlude. Within a generation, the American Revolution had removed the southern portion.

In the newly independent United States, the symbols of British governance soon began to wither. In the rest, British North America, they would long endure. In many ways, they dominate our country to this day. Among the thirteen provinces and territories, for instance, eleven shields and ten flags contain British symbolism.

The following are the key flags of British North America and the highest-profile examples of their legacy.

Flags of the British Kingdoms

Determining the identity of national flags during the British era is less problematic than for the French period. In Britain, flags emerged from purely royal standards much earlier than in France, albeit unofficially. This reflects the more constitutional nature of its governance from an early age.

On the other hand, the term "British" is itself complicated. Indeed, it had no legal meaning prior to 1603, when James VI of Scotland also became

James I of England, putting the two countries under one monarch. Still, they remained legally separate realms.

For the Kingdom of England, the national flag was the St. George's Cross (see Figure 17). The perpendicular red on white design had emerged during the Crusades—George was the soldier's saint—and had been the general English flag since at least the thirteenth century. It was this banner that flew over John Cabot's ship, *Matthew*.[29]

The early British presence in Newfoundland, Quebec, and Rupert's Land came under the auspices of the Kingdom of England, but Nova Scotia was founded as a colony of the Kingdom of Scotland. Its national flag was the St. Andrew's Cross (see Figure 18). Its diagonal white on blue design may be of even older vintage than its English counterpart. The saltire (diagonal cross) was chosen to represent the way in which Scotland's patron saint had been crucified.

James VI/I was anxious to fully merge his two kingdoms and, three years later, launched a new flag for all of Great Britain. Thus, the first Union Jack (see Figure 19), occasionally and more properly called the Union Flag, was created. Both his English and Scottish subjects initially disliked the design and, more importantly, they rejected James's political objective.

The English and the Scottish did, however, accept James's directive to fly the Union Jack, in addition to their own national flags, on the ships of both realms. And it gradually caught on. In fact, it became so common that in 1634, Charles I thought it necessary to restrict its usage to royal vessels only. The Union Jack remains forbidden on non-military ships to this day.

In 1707, the English and Scottish Parliaments finally consented to create the United Kingdom of Great Britain. It was at this point that the Union Jack became a truly national flag, although authorization for its use remained quite limited. It was also under this flag that Canada fell fully under British control.

A half-century after the conquest of New France, the Union Jack evolved. In 1801, the Kingdom of Ireland, long ruled by English monarchs, was incorporated into the United Kingdom. Consequently, the St. Patrick's Cross was added to the previous design (see Figure 20).

The choice was not without controversy. The red saltire on white had little previous use as an Irish national symbol. It was also a peculiar emblem because, while Patrick is Ireland's patron saint, he was not crucified. No doubt the selection had been driven by its ease of integration into the existing pattern.[30]

Whether an authentic emblem of the United Kingdom of Great Britain and Ireland, this second Union Jack is used to symbolize the period of British rule in Canada's coat of arms. It was, in fact, the flag usually flown over British government and military establishments. Today, it is universally treated as the British national flag, although it has never actually been legislated as such.

Some additional points are worth mentioning. First, all three countries remain represented in the banner, although since 1922, the United Kingdom has included only Northern Ireland. Loosely based on Ulster, it is historically a mere province of the former kingdom. Second, Wales is not represented. That is because it was traditionally classed as a principality within the Kingdom of England. Finally, Scotland itself retains the original, sky-blue colour of the St. Andrew's Cross. The blue on the Union Jack has darkened considerably over the centuries, which has often occurred with blue flags.[31]

British Ensigns

The four "national crosses"—St. George's, St. Andrew's, Union 1707, and Union 1801—were by no means the only British flags to fly over colonial Canada. For instance, the flags of republican England, the short-lived Commonwealth of 1649–1660, would likely have appeared in both Newfoundland and Nova Scotia.[32] Those banners, however, were of no lasting consequence.

As with New France, the most common and most consequential flags in British North America were the ones on ships. The experience in both realms had strong parallels. Both the principal French and British ensigns were red, blue, and white, and generally dominated by their national crosses. Both also frequently formed the basis of the regimental flags used in these colonies. And both provoked a sense of attachment to the mother countries, making them the source of much future flag development.

Up to the early 1600s, British ships had a range of ensigns that were typically marked by horizontal stripes with the national flag in the canton (the upper left rectangular section). After that, the stripes gave way to solid colours. These have subsequently gone through three incarnations, beginning with the English or Scottish cross in the canton, replaced in 1707 by the original Union one, and finally, in 1801 by the contemporary version.

The first and most important of these solid-coloured flags was the Red Ensign (see Figure 21). Until 1864, the Red Ensign served as both a naval flag—often the preeminent one—and a merchant flag. After that time, it became restricted at sea to commercial ships, while its use on land was largely unfettered. Nicknamed the "Red Duster," this British flag would have been seen more often in North America than any other.

The Blue Ensign (see Figure 22) was also long employed on warships. In 1864, however, it was assigned its present role as the flag of the Royal Navy Reserve and of non-naval government vessels. In the latter case, each department or agency adds its own insignia. In 1865, British colonial governments were given permission to create unique Blue Ensigns for their own ships by adding their local shield or crest.

It appears that the first use of this new prerogative in British North America was by the federal government shortly after Confederation.[33] Yet, despite being an authorized flag, the Canadian Blue Ensign never caught the public imagination like its Australian or New Zealand counterpart. As a result, it was seldom used in Canada for anything other than its official purpose.

Like France's *Pavillon blanc*, Britain's White Ensign (see Figure 23) evolved a distinctive design, which in this case includes the full St. George's Cross. This ensign was at first a lower-ranking naval flag. That changed when Admiral Nelson famously promoted it to all British ships at the Battle of Trafalgar. In 1864, it officially became, with only a few exceptions, the exclusive flag of the Royal Navy.

Canada never had its own version of the British White Ensign. Nevertheless, it long served as the principal flag of the Royal Canadian Navy, with the Canadian Blue Ensign also flown to signify the country.[34] As well, the White Ensign was occasionally used as the basis for national flag proposals.[35]

British Colonial Flags

While various royal standards, national flags, coloured ensigns, and regimental banners flew in British North America, neither the area nor any part of it had its own, official, pre-Confederation flag. Still, some British colonies and territories began to regularly use specific local banners. They initially arose in the five original British jurisdictions.

These early "Canadian" flags first appeared in Rupert's Land, courtesy of its governing authority, the London-headquartered Hudson's Bay Company (HBC). In fact, the company had a range of banners. Often employed were its Governor's Standard—the HBC coat of arms on a white background—and the Union Jack, which it had special authorization to fly. The most important flag, however, was the HBC Red Ensign (see Figure 24).

The HBC has always maintained that this flag was authorized in 1682 by its founder, Prince Rupert, cousin of Charles II, in his capacity as vice admiral of the Royal Navy. If that is so, then the flag passed through all three phases in the canton. Yet, we do not know when its usage really began, and there is little evidence of it prior to the early nineteenth century. In any case, the HBC Red Ensign has long been identified with Rupert's Land in popular lore. It can still be seen flying on the company's historical sites today.[36]

Strictly speaking, the HBC Red Ensign was not the flag of Rupert's Land. It was the flag of the company, placed above its establishments. Nevertheless, in the view of the United Kingdom, the HBC was the ruling authority there, making its banner effectively a territorial one.

The situation in the North-Western Territory was much fuzzier. The area, defined loosely as any UK claim not in another jurisdiction, had no designated government. The HBC's principal rival became so by default, as the first organization to establish a British presence in the region. Naturally, it created its own North West Company (NWC) Red Ensign (see Figure 25).

The actions of the Montreal-based NWC were not entirely proper. While merchants had been known to sometimes add their insignia to a Red Ensign, the NWC had no authorization to do so, just as it had no authorization to make itself an administration. Its assertion of authority set off a gradually escalating civil war. It ended only when the British government forced the NWC to merge with the HBC in 1821. Thereafter, the HBC Red Ensign became the common flag of both territories until they were purchased by the young Dominion of Canada in 1870.

The upshot is that even before Confederation and the creation of the Canadian Red Ensign,[37] that design had become a British North American template. Again, this is not surprising. The Red Ensign was not just the most common British flag in colonial Canada. Its dominant red was seen by British-Canadians as their national colour, much as French-Canadians had identified with white. And, once again, that was reflected in the standard colour of the infantrymen.

Developments in Canada were paralleled in the one part of British North America that long stayed out of Confederation: Newfoundland. Newfoundland has a long and interesting flag history. Besides hosting the banners of a range of nations and governors, the colony, like Quebec, began to develop its own local designs in the nineteenth century. Most prominent among those was the Newfoundland Tricolour, a flag of green, white, and pink[38] vertical stripes. Its resemblance to the future banner of Ireland was not coincidental, as the most obvious interpretation of it—green for Catholics, British pink (versus Irish orange) for Protestants, and white for peace between them—is identical.

However, as the colony approached dominion status, an official local flag emerged, the Newfoundland Red Ensign (see Figure 26). Adopted in 1904, the banner was distinguished by the colony's seal. It displayed a fisherman being presented to the goddess Britannia by Mercury, the Roman deity of commerce. Surrounding the scene are, in Latin, the words "Newfoundland—These Gifts I Bring to Thee." Strictly speaking, this was a merchant flag but, as in Canada, it was used more widely. Likewise, the corresponding Newfoundland Blue Ensign was rarely employed beyond government vessels.

Once Newfoundland's independence began to fade, so did its distinctive ensigns. In 1931, with the country inching back to British colonial status,

Newfoundland adopted the Union Jack as its formal flag. It remained so until 1980, when a stylized version that incorporated other symbolism was approved. Although the Newfoundland ensigns were not completely discontinued until 1965, they largely disappeared after the colony joined Canada. What has not vanished is the Newfoundland Tricolour, which has become a symbol of residual Newfoundland nationalism.

The Red Ensign was not the inspiration for pre-Confederation flag development in either Quebec or Nova Scotia. Quebec's vexillological traditions are French in origin.[39] Nova Scotia's are uniquely Scottish, giving birth to Canada's oldest provincial flag and one of its most admired.[40]

The flag of Nova Scotia is derived from its coat of arms, first granted in 1625. It shows the royal shield of Scotland over an inverted St. Andrew's Cross (see Figure 27). Reversing colours in this manner is a common method of illustrating descendance. However, the flag does not date back to the seventeenth century, despite claims to the contrary. The evidence suggests that the shield was not converted into a banner until 1858. Yet, this flag seems to have been flown only sporadically in the decades following Confederation.

Why did sightings of the flag become scarce in those years? We can only speculate. One possible explanation might be found in the initial unpopularity of Confederation in Nova Scotia. Virtually all politicians supporting it, both federally and provincially, lost in the elections of 1867. It is against this backdrop that, in 1868, Nova Scotia was granted a new and very different coat of arms. As provincehood gradually came to be embraced, it is possible that the older shield and flag came to be identified with separatism.

Nevertheless, the original arms made a comeback, likely in no small part because they are so attractive and meaningful. In 1929, the province succeeded in having them restored by royal warrant. At the same time, the old banner became widely used and regularly employed for official purposes. Still, it was not actually made the official flag of the province in legislation until 2013.

Provincial Legacy Flags

The flags of Nova Scotia and Quebec are by far the oldest among the provinces. It was not until 1960 that the other provinces and territories began to devise their own banners. Most of these—the Northwest Territories and Nunavut are the exceptions—borrow symbolism and flag elements from the British period.

That said, only two of these newer banners, like those of Nova Scotia and Quebec, are explicitly based on historical flags. These are the flags of Ontario and Manitoba. Once again, both are based on the Red Ensign.

As detailed in the next chapter, the identification of British-Canadians with the Red Ensign only deepened after Confederation. That flag, with the addition of Canada's evolving shield, became the unofficial banner of the country. When the national flag was finally adopted in 1965, it was opposed by a large minority of the population in English-speaking Canada. Most of those had argued for the Canadian Red Ensign instead.

It is in this context that Ontario and Manitoba adopted their flags. It was not merely the rejection of the Canadian Red Ensign as the national flag that led to their decisions. It was also the refusal to give an official role of any kind to that popular and historical banner.[41]

The flag of Ontario (see Figure 28) simply substituted the province's shield for the national one. That shield was one of four assigned to the original members of Confederation by Queen Victoria. It consists of the St. George's Cross over three conjoined gold maple leaves on a green background. The former represents Ontario's English-speaking heritage, while the latter is the official symbol of the province.

The flag of Manitoba (see Figure 29) consists of the province's shield on a similarly "defaced" Red Ensign (meaning an element has been added to distinguish it). Manitoba's coat of arms officially dates from 1905, although the basic design was used informally after its admission to Canada in 1870. The pattern of the shield parallels that of Ontario's: the St. George's Cross over a brown bison on a rock, also against a green background. That symbolic animal is inherited from the flag of Louis Riel's rebel government of 1869–1870.[42]

Vexillologists have tended to be critical of these flags on two grounds.[43] The first is that the distinguishing elements, the provincial shields, are relatively small and indistinct. Unless one is close to the flag, it is not readily apparent to which jurisdiction these banners belong. That would seem to be a valid complaint.

The second critique is more dubious. It is that the basic design, the Red Ensign, is essentially the flag of another country. This ignores the historical context. Red Ensigns of various types have flown over Canada for centuries.

For that reason, the design has become a distinct symbol of Canada in the eyes of many. Nowhere is this truer than in Ontario and Manitoba, where such flags have waved the longest, from the earliest days of the fur trade.

I have said that British symbolism is still a dominant element of state emblems in much of the country. That assertion holds beyond the provincial level of government, and it is particularly true in the case of the Red Ensign. For instance, the Red Ensign has been the basis of many Canadian regimental colours, as have the Blue Ensign and other British flags.

Along these lines, Alberta's Tsuut'ina First Nation, whose reserve is only a few hundred yards from my residence, is particularly noteworthy. That community's official flag is also based on the Red Ensign, with its local badge added to the fly (the outer part). This is just one example of the connections, real and symbolic, that are maintained between Indigenous peoples and the Crown.[44]

The Flag of the United States

Back in 1986, a controversy arose around new notes issued by the Bank of Canada. Citizens were initially outraged at what appeared on the bills to be the American flag flying over Parliament. However, careful examination would show that the banner depicted, in fact, was the Canadian Red Ensign.

In truth, the whole affair was a rare demonstration of historical fidelity in official Ottawa. The scene on the bills illustrated the Victoria Tower of the original legislature, which was destroyed by fire in 1917—not the current Peace Tower. It also correctly showed the flag that flew over Parliament in the early years of Confederation.

Yet, at the heart of this misunderstanding is a greater historical truth. The flag of the United States shares its roots with earlier Canadian ones. Those roots are to be found in the Red Ensign.

Let me demonstrate this, starting with a drawing of the Red Ensign at the beginning of the American Revolution: the Red Ensign of 1707 (see Figure 30). For ease of comparison, this is shown with the same dimensions as the modern flag of the United States. As previously noted, flag shapes have changed over the centuries. The Red Ensign of that era was more squarish, with the canton typically occupying much less than the one-quarter of the design that it does today.

It is a small step from that Red Ensign to the first national flag of the United States, adopted in late 1775. Known as the Grand Union Flag or Continental Colors (see Figure 31), it contained the older Union Jack in the canton with the field broken up by six white horizontal stripes sewn onto a readily available Red Duster. The resulting thirteen stripes were a clear reference to the thirteen rebel colonies.

It has been noted that this flag closely resembled the banner of the East India Company. That corporation was unique in maintaining the kind of striped ensign common before the early seventeenth century. Its stripes, an odd number between nine to fifteen, also alternated in red and white. However, that flag was not flown on this side of the Atlantic, where the company, having carried the infamous cargo of the Boston Tea Party, was distinctly unpopular. Thus, the likeness is almost certainly coincidental. The Red Ensign, by contrast, was already being used as the basis of some local colonial flags and rebel militia banners.

The Continental Colours perfectly illustrated the initial aspirations of the aggrieved colonists: that the King would recognize and accommodate their historical rights as British subjects. When it quickly became apparent that this would not happen, the aim of the Revolution became political independence. That, in turn, required a new flag.

In 1777, the Continental Congress authorized the original Stars & Stripes (see Figure 32). A constellation of thirteen white stars on a blue background would replace the Union Jack in the canton. It would be some time before the arrangement of these stars, their number of points, and other aspects of the pattern became standardized. One major design element of the flag would even be transformed as it evolved.

The original intention had been to increase the number of stars and stripes as new states joined the union. Accordingly, in 1795, the number of both was increased to fifteen. It was to this flag that Francis Scott Key dedicated "The Star-Spangled Banner." Nevertheless, by 1818, when Congress faced the prospect of a flag with twenty states, it decided to limit the number of stripes to the original thirteen, thereafter increasing only the number of stars. Thus, today's national flag of the United States contains fifty stars but only thirteen stripes (see Figure 33).

British flag traditions have not entirely died in the United States. The most notable example is the state of Hawaii, which still employs a striped British ensign. To the north, however, in the territory originally controlled by New France and the HBC, the Red Ensign and other British flags continued to dominate. After Confederation in 1867, they became central in a series of national debates about the appropriate design for a Canadian national flag.

3

The Flag of Canada and its Emergence

AS EARLY AS the 1600s, a distinctly New World symbol emerged in the outposts of New France and British North America: the beaver. The industrious little animal was the most important product of both the French and British fur trades. Its coat was long desired by affluent European consumers. With a habitat covering the continent (save the polar region), it was also omnipresent.

However, the beaver was eclipsed as the preeminent Canadian symbol in the decades following 1821. That was when the HBC absorbed the NWC, assuring that London, not Montreal, would be the headquarters of the fur trade. Besides, there were doubts about whether any rodent possessed the majesty sufficient for a paramount national emblem.[45]

The ascendency of the beaver passed to the maple leaf. Evidence suggests that the new symbol arose independently among both Francophones and Anglophones by the early 1800s.[46] The leaf of the sugar maple was appealing because of both its bold shape and its multiple colours. The main drawback—it grew only in the southeastern corner of British North America—made little difference. That is where almost all the colonial population then lived.

This begs an obvious question: If the dominant Canadian symbol emerged so long ago, why was a national flag based upon it so long in coming? The answer lies in Canadian identity itself. Canada transitioned from a French to a British entity at one moment in eighteenth-century history. By contrast, Canada became independent from Britain through a gradual evolution. That process, combined with the cultural complexity of the country, meant that the ultimate choice of a national banner ran up against both differing and evolving concepts of Canada.

It is not my intention to recount here the path by which Canada progressed from a group of separate British colonies to a united and sovereign state. Suffice it to say that it was long, multi-phased, and a combination of both Canadian-pull and British-push. However, one date stands out. In 1867, four of the provinces of British North America created a federation and, through it, established their own national government.[47]

Within six years, virtually all of British North America had been brought into the new Dominion of Canada (see Figure 34).[48] The basic constitutional framework and key institutions of today's country were in place. Indeed, despite our relative youth, Canada has at present one of the world's longest-enduring political systems.

It is against this backdrop that Canada's flag debates, or, more precisely, four rounds of flag debates, occurred. They took place in Parliament, through media, and at private institutions. Over the decades, they produced thousands of proposals. This article will focus on the surprisingly small number of designs that had a significant distribution and following.

The Flag Debate 1867-1918

The first official flags of the new Dominion of Canada were authorized in 1870. They centred on the original shield, which was just a quartering of the shields of the four founding provinces (see Figure 35). These had been developed during the planning of Confederation and granted by Queen Victoria the following year. Most notable was the inclusion of a sprig of three maple leaves on the arms of both Ontario (in gold) and Quebec (in green). The leaves were typically fifteen-pointed.

Except for Ontario's, these shields are not the same as today's provincial coats of arms. Quebec's government changed the top part (the "chief") of its shield in 1939 to show three gold fleurs-de-lis on blue, the traditional mark of royal France. Queen Victoria had modified that design, substituting two blue fleurs-de-lis on gold, to assure Napoleon III that she was not making a claim to the French throne. Nova Scotia's shield was completely revised in 1929.[49] New Brunswick's varies only slightly, principally because, since 1965, the ship has sailed in the opposite (and more heraldically appropriate) direction.

Among the new flags with the four-province shield was one for the governor general. In it, the Dominion shield was surrounded by a wreath of green maple leaves, surmounted by a crown, and placed on a white plate in the centre of the Union Jack. The flags of the lieutenant governors were similar, with their respective provincial shields, but without the crown.

Another authorized flag was the Canadian Blue Ensign. It was a Blue Ensign with the unadorned shield in the fly. This banner was reserved for federal government vessels, and it was rarely used for other purposes.[50]

There was no sanctioned Canadian Red Ensign, but such a flag also appeared in the early years of Confederation (see Figure 36). In fact, it was used by Prime Minister John A. Macdonald as the de facto banner of the new Dominion. Almost from the outset, it flew above the Parliament buildings in Ottawa with his blessing.

Getting formal recognition of the flag was a more difficult matter. Technically, it only had to be authorized at sea, and Macdonald sought to have the Canadian Red Ensign designated as the flag of Canada's merchant marine. The request was refused by the British Admiralty in 1875.

Macdonald tried again in 1890. He would be backed by an active grassroots campaign to encourage the flying of the banner. The prime minister also had the support of Governor General Lord Stanley. The Canadian Red Ensign, Stanley told the British government, "is one which has come to be considered as the recognized flag of the Dominion, both ashore and afloat."[51] In 1892, the year after Macdonald's death, the Admiralty gave his flag official status.

That might have led to the recognition of the Canadian Red Ensign as the country's national flag—if not for one enormous problem: There was no agreement on its design. I am not referring only to the many different patterns manufacturers created by putting wreaths, crowns, plates, beavers, and various other trimmings around the shield. Even the shield itself was subject to multiple versions.

The obvious challenge with the shield was its exclusion of the provinces joining after 1867. Flag-makers tried to rectify this by creating designs that included the arms of the new provinces and sometimes even the territories. For provinces where there were no official arms, the shields had simply been invented by private citizens.

The dilemma is underscored by the famous Macdonald poster from his final election campaign in 1891. The "Old Leader" waves his "Old Flag" (see Figure 37). But it is an ordinary Red Ensign, without any shield at all, even though Canada already had seven provinces. Sir John A. thus sidesteps the controversy.

By 1905, Confederation included nine provinces, and, within two years, all their arms (see Figure 38) had been officially granted. Flags with this full range were common (see Figure 39), even if the provincial ordering was often incorrect and, once again, other embellishments were included. Note, however, that only the plain, four-province version ever had any official standing.

Obviously, a nine-province version was painfully overcrowded, containing almost two dozen design elements. There were proposals to simplify it. A few prominent people even suggested replacing the shield with the maple leaf. It could be in either green or yellow (heraldic gold) and either alone or in a group of three. However, these ideas seem to have attracted remarkably little following. Perhaps this was because the real rival to the Canadian Red Ensign was an even simpler design: the Union Jack itself.

Though steadily gaining autonomy in this period, Canada remained fully a part of the British Empire. That is what Canadians of all backgrounds had desired ever since the American Revolution. Belonging to "the greatest Empire the world has ever known" was their sense of security opposite a huge, sometimes hostile neighbour. Indeed, it was the principal reason why such disparate regions and peoples had come together in Confederation—their fear of the victorious Union army after the US Civil War.

Thus, the purest flag of British nationhood had a following in Canada from the beginning. Its ranks experienced a huge boost in 1897. During Queen Victoria's Diamond Jubilee, the Union Jack completed its transition from royal banner to national flag. It was waved with abandon during the celebrations, occurring as they did at the height of the Empire's power and prestige.

The first great Canadian flag debate had begun in earnest. On one side was the Canadian Red Ensign, a flag representing (even if design-challenged) the country's distinct identity. On the other was the Union Jack, standing for a wider loyalty.

The turning point came in 1899 with the start of the Boer War or, more properly, the South African War. Anglophone Canadians made an important contribution to the ultimate British success. With their pride of place in the Empire swelling, flag-waving nationalists increasingly made the Union Jack their banner of choice. By 1904, it had replaced the Canadian Red Ensign atop the Parliament buildings in Ottawa.

Ironically, it was the Quebec nationalist (then Liberal MP) Henri Bourassa who spoke up against the demotion of "the Canadian flag."[52]

Among Francophones, the conquest of the Boers was viewed differently. In Quebec (and elsewhere in the world), it came to be seen as the crushing of a small, independent people by British brute force. So, as Anglophones began to downplay the Canadian Red Ensign in favour of the Union Jack, Francophones started searching for their own banner. They would soon choose the *Carillon Sacré-Coeur*.[53]

It has been thought that purely Canadian designs did not appear until later flag debates. However, my brother, Grant, discovered a lapel button from 1899 advocating an "Independence of Canada" flag (see Figure 40). It is not too many steps from that design to our eventual national flag. However, there is little to suggest that this or any proposal like it made much of an impact at the time.[54]

The Union Jack-Canadian Red Ensign debate continued into World War I, but it was never fully resolved. Much of the argument revolved around which was the "official national flag." In truth, neither was. One was formally the flag of British governmental institutions; the other was legally the ensign of Canadian commercial ships. In practice, both flags were commonly used, with the Union Jack regarded by most of the population as the national flag and the Canadian Red Ensign championed by those who wished to stress their autonomous status.

The Flag Debate 1918-1945

The "war to end all wars" transformed virtually every aspect of society. It permanently weakened the British Empire. This put in motion the process that moved Canada from a self-governing entity to a truly independent country. It also changed North America geopolitically. Americans had joined Canadians on the battlefields in 1917, transforming a relationship of wary neighbours into one of trusting allies.

The country's march to full sovereignty began in earnest with distinct Canadian representation at the Versailles treaty talks. However, it had been foreshadowed by Canada's increasingly separate identity during the war itself. At Vimy Ridge, in particular, an army led by a Canadian, drawn from all parts of the country, and waving both the Union Jack and four-province Canadian Red Ensign, had won a spectacular victory.

Naturally, this new nation would begin to search for genuinely national symbols. The early focus was on developing a national coat of arms, one that would rise above a mere patchwork of provincial shields. In 1921, one was approved. Its shield contains five elements: the royal shields of England, Scotland, Ireland, and France, along with the three conjoined maple leaves to represent Canada itself (see Figure 41).

The design is attractive, but it is a bit hard to explain. If it is intended to be a royal shield, then the inclusion of a symbol for France makes little sense, as the British/Canadian monarch does not claim the French throne. If it is to instead represent the state's founding nations, then the inclusion of Ireland is odd as that kingdom did not plant a colony in Canada (notwithstanding the large number of Irish settlers). If it is to represent the peoples of Canada broadly, then it has no elements to acknowledge anyone outside of the British Isles or France, not even Indigenous nations.

The use of maple leaves for Canada was, of course, already well established. It had been further entrenched by their ubiquitous presence on the country's uniforms during World War I. It is about this time that the points of the leaves were reduced to thirteen, although the renderings often varied. Displaying them in a group of three was aesthetic, not symbolic. As with the shields of Ontario and Quebec, it had been felt that a single leaf was too plain, whereas nine (for the provinces) would have been too cluttered.

More contentious on Canada's new arms was the colour of the leaves. They had been drawn in green on *argent* (a silver or white background). Green was already the colour assigned to Quebec, although on *or* (a gold or yellow background). Yet the wreath and mantling of the arms, the elements normally linked to the state colours, were in red and white. And the lion on the crest is holding a single red maple leaf.

It appears that the officials who designed the arms wanted red and white to be the colours of Canada. Why, then, was the Canadian symbol on the shield shown in green and white? The answer, it seems, is that those around Robert Borden and Arthur Meighen, and perhaps even one of those prime ministers, intervened to make the change. In their minds, green was the colour of youth and life, while a red maple leaf was one in a stage of decay and death.

Why would the designers have designated red and white as the colours of Canada? No precise explanation was given, beyond vague allusions to blood and snow. It should be noted, however, that the first royal medal after Confederation—for the successful defence against the Fenian Raids—had a red-white-red ribbon. These became the colours of the Royal Military College in Kingston, as well as its flag.

The next logical step in this exercise was the substitution of the new coat of arms on Canada's flags. This was officially mandated within a year for the Governor General's Standard, the Canadian Blue Ensign, and the Canadian Red Ensign (see Figure 42). However, the federal government did not merely alter the merchant ensign; it also raised its status.

In 1924, Ottawa instructed that the Canadian Red Ensign be flown on all government establishments abroad. This, it could be argued, was an extension of existing practice. Even if the Union Jack had usually been employed as the country's flag at home, the Canadian Red Ensign had often been utilized to distinguish Canada from Britain in the wider world.

This, however, appears to have been only a first step in Ottawa's plans. In 1925, the cabinet struck a committee of senior officials to quietly study options for a "distinctive flag" for Canada. When the exercise became public knowledge, all hell broke loose.

The government was lambasted for the private and unrepresentative nature of the committee. This had not been a problem when the coat of arms was being developed. But a coat of arms is not a flag and does not generate the same passions. Supporters of the Union Jack and the Canadian Red Ensign attacked the idea of even examining the issue.

Prime Minister Mackenzie King was in a precarious parliamentary situation and faced an upcoming election. He cut a predictable and hasty retreat. The committee was scrapped and a promise was made that, should the issue ever arise again, it would go to Parliament first.

However, the issue did not go away. Parliament saw a half dozen debates on flag resolutions as the 1920s and 1930s progressed. These deliberations became more frequent after 1931, when the Statute of Westminster confirmed Canada's sovereignty in law. It was also the same year that the Governor General's Standard was overhauled.

The new version of the GG's flag featured the removal of the Union Jack background in favour of plain blue. This pattern would eventually be repeated in the flags of all the lieutenant governors.[55] But, oddly, Mackenzie King later employed the Union Jack, with a green maple leaf in the centre, as a prime ministerial flag on one occasion.[56]

Alongside the political debates were flag discussions and design contests in periodicals, as well as enthusiasts publishing their own proposals. Few of these aspiring national banners got any traction, but they embraced some common themes. They were invariably more striking and less intricate in symbolism than the Canadian Red Ensign. They also tended to be oriented toward the concept of two founding nations.

That seems to be what the aborted officials' committee of 1925 had in mind all along. In 1939, the federal government unfurled a new banner, the "Canadian Active Service Force Ensign," generally known as the Canadian Battle Flag (see Figure 43). Created by Colonel Fortescue Duguid, it did, in fact, date back to the committee.[57] And its design was focused on the two-founding-nations concept.

The Canadian Battle Flag was cleverly engineered. With the Union Jack on one side and an oval version of the royal French shield over a white background on the other, it could be interpreted as a two-nations flag. But it could also be seen as simply a Canadian variant of the British White Ensign.

Yet, the most important feature of the new flag was the three conjoined maple leaves dominating its centre. A purely Canadian symbol was being given pre-eminence on a national banner for the first time. Note also that the leaves were displayed in red, even though they remained green on the coat of arms. This was more evidence of the hand of officialdom in the design.

The Canadian Battle Flag was the first serious competitor to the Union Jack and Canadian Red Ensign. It helped that its foremost promoter was the federal government. Initially, the banner accompanied the country's army as it headed overseas in World War II. But Ottawa looked for occasions to publicly display the design, as King was said to be fond of it. Specimens of various sizes were produced and can be tracked down to this day.

Nevertheless, the new flag did not get the traction the government had hoped for, and its war use was gradually displaced by the Canadian Red Ensign. Having the maple leaves as the dominant emblem had been welcomed, but the layout of the Canadian Battle Flag seemed otherwise cluttered. It may also be that the two-nations symbolism was beginning to fall flat among both Anglophones and Francophones.

Anglophones who valued the British connection saw no equivalency in the French relationship. After all, Canada had essentially British political institutions, not French ones. The association with France was largely historical, whereas the connection to Britain was deep and enduring. And although the country had passed from an autonomous entity within the Empire to an independent member of the Commonwealth, many English-Canadians still saw "Britishness" as part of their political identity.

In contrast, being French was a cultural identity for Francophones, not a political one. Their homeland had long ceased to be France; it was Canada. French-Canadians already had their own flag in the *Carillon Sacré-Coeur*, which was by then the official banner of the *Société Saint-Jean-Baptiste*.[58] For a flag of the country itself, they seemed inclined to strictly Canadian symbolism.

For these reasons, the failure of the Canadian Battle Flag effectively marked the end of a two-founding-nations model for a national flag. While it is true that such proposals continued to be advanced into the final deliberations of the 1960s, they were never again serious contenders.

The second flag debate petered out as the fighting in Europe intensified. It left the Canadian Red Ensign on an equal footing with the Union Jack. The new coat of arms had ended uncertainty around its design, and it was being used widely for official purposes. It also benefited from the country's new sovereign status and the shift in perspective that implied. And while the Canadian Red Ensign only marginally displayed the independent nation's maple-leaf symbol, the bolder alternative, the Canadian Battle Flag, had clearly failed to supplant it.

The Flag Debate 1945–1957

World War II fundamentally altered Canada's place in the world. It was not just that the country declared and pursued its own war effort. In a reversal of historical roles, it was Canada helping to save the United Kingdom during the Battle of Britain in 1940. That same year, Canada entered into a mutual defence agreement with the United States, which henceforth became its most critical ally. The implications of this new strategic positioning were not entirely understood at the time.

In any case, a new flag debate broke out almost as soon as the fighting ended. The groundwork was being laid during the war itself. As WWII progressed, the Canadian Red Ensign increasingly dislodged not only the Canadian Battle Flag, but also the Union Jack and other service ensigns, as the flag of the Canadian war effort and of Canadian nationhood generally. Canadian officials would invariably use the banner when they found themselves at allied meetings.

Shortly after the final surrender of the Axis powers in 1945, cabinet authorized the flying of the Canadian Red Ensign over all federal government buildings "until such time as action is taken by Parliament for the formal adoption of a national flag."[59] While a few supporters of the Union Jack vehemently objected, even the opposition Conservatives overwhelmingly supported the decision. Indeed, they began to press Prime Minister King to make the Canadian Red Ensign the official national flag.

This time, King decided to be proactive. He launched a joint parliamentary committee to study the flag question. It received over 2,500 suggestions, more than ten times the number that had appeared in 1925. Union Jacks, stars, fleurs-de-lis, beavers, crowns, and/or crosses were contained in many of the submissions. However, maple leaves were far and away the dominant symbol proposed, being present in some 60 percent of designs.

This input seemed to confirm King's instincts. He believed that the country was gravitating toward the Canadian Red Ensign, but that it wanted stronger, more immediately recognizable, Canadian symbolism. From behind the curtain, he pushed the committee toward his preference.

It would turn out to be a new Canadian Red Ensign with the coat of arms replaced by a single, large, gold maple leaf (see Figure 44). Recall that similar designs had been mooted as far back as the 1890s. In this case, a very "leafy" version of the maple was proposed, which was both odd and unattractive.[60]

Public opinion was evolving more quickly than the wily old prime minister realized. A grassroots campaign had emerged to advocate for an altogether different alternative: the proposal of the National Flag League (see Figure 45). It was actually the project of two organizations, the largely Francophone *Ligue du drapeau national* and the mainly Anglophone Native Sons of Canada.

The National Flag League offered a clear rationale for its choice of colours. Red, it explained, was the traditional colour of British-Canadians, and white was that of French-Canadians. This seems far more likely than anything officials had admitted when they had pushed the combination back in 1921. It was a compelling, yet subtle way to reflect a two-nations heritage. The sole symbol on the banner was a single Canadian maple leaf in green. That colour was to represent the land, and, in any event, the coat of arms still sported green leaves.

Through 1946, the parliamentary committee moved toward consensus on the simplified Canadian Red Ensign. However, close to half the public submissions were supporting the National Flag League option. The federal government was then hit with a broadside. The Legislative Assembly of Quebec pre-emptively voted to reject any flag that included any sign of colonialism. It was a transparent attack on the inclusion of the Union Jack in the design.

King ultimately declined to move the committee's recommendation forward. He sensed that public opinion was not merely divided, but that it risked becoming polarized. As he had done in 1925, the prime minister moved to end the parliamentary debate. While the debate would continue in the country, King would have nothing more to do with it.

Over time, a fascinating dynamic had unfolded around the Canadian Red Ensign. In the early 1900s, as Anglophones were subordinating it to the Union Jack, Francophones were prepared to support it. In the 1920s, with Anglophones raising its status, Francophones had concluded it could only be tolerated with the inclusion of equal French symbolism. And now, just as Anglophones were fully embracing it, Francophones deemed it unacceptable. This dynamic had prevented a national flag from emerging in Ottawa, yet it had led to consensus around a provincial flag in Quebec.

The alternative, a model based on purely Canadian symbolism, was just as far from consensus. But the National Flag League design had, with little high-profile backing, emerged as the single biggest challenger to the traditional patterns. It would also prove to be the unmistakeable forerunner of our eventual national flag.

The Flag Debate 1957-1965

A key step in the final flag debate was undertaken before it truly began by people who really did not want it to happen. In 1957, the newly elected Conservative government of Prime Minister John Diefenbaker made significant changes to Canada's coat of arms. For one thing, the Irish harp was given a simplified form. For another, the maple leaves were finally changed from green to red (see Figure 46).

The decision had the effect of removing any ambiguity about Canada's national colours. It was soon reflected in various flags and other insignia. For example, it has determined all versions of the Canadian flags of members of the royal family. They are essentially cloth versions of the shield, often with a personal mark or crest added. Of course, the change in the shield also necessitated further modification to the Canadian Red Ensign (see Figure 47).

Meanwhile, the postwar years were witnessing profound shifts in Western societies. By the 1960s, wide gaps were evident in the worldview of those who had come of age before and during the war versus those who were younger. In Canada, these social changes were overlaid by unique dynamics among both the Anglophone and Francophone populations.

Among Anglophones, the decline of the connection to the United Kingdom was evident. The British Empire was dissolving, and the Commonwealth, while it remained an important global association, was simply not as relevant to political consciousness in Canada. At the same time, the new relationship with the United States created a mixed reaction. The American alliance gave English-Canadians their greatest level of national security ever. But this closeness also threatened their sense of separate identity in a way the British relationship never did.

For its part, French-Canadian life was undergoing some of the most radical social change in the world. Particularly in Quebec, Francophones were moving from one of the most traditionally pious peoples on the planet to one of the most thoroughly secularized. And French-Canadian identity in its heartland was rapidly morphing into explicit Quebec nationalism.

The new consciousness of Anglophones was bound to find expression in a renewed Canadian nationalism and a rekindled interest in national symbols such as the flag. The new nationalism of Francophones implied the potential risk of Quebec separatism. The Liberal Party, whose electoral fortunes depended on Quebec, was especially alert to that risk. In any case, both developments led the federal Liberal leader, Lester Pearson, to make the adoption of an official national flag a firm commitment as early as 1960.

The flag debate that followed Pearson's election as prime minister was the shortest and the most intense in Canadian history. Increasing public discussion had begun to produce the normal flow of proposals. However, Pearson put the cat among the pigeons when, in May 1964, he produced his own preferred alternative. It was quickly, usually pejoratively, dubbed the Pearson Pennant (see Figure 48).

Pearson's flag was anything but strange. Its principal feature was the three-red-maple-leaves sprig from the coat of arms. The prime minister, in his quest for an exclusively Canadian design, had borrowed a simplified version of Duguid's original Canadian Battle Flag. But Pearson believed that the symbol on a plain white background would appear too empty. He had thus chosen a variant created by Lieutenant Commander Alan Beddoe, whose blue sidebars were meant to reflect Canada's "sea to sea" national motto.[61]

The blue bars were controversial in more heraldically orthodox quarters. They were not the traditional "wavy lines" way of depicting water bodies (although Pearson's intent was metaphoric, not geographic). More notably, they departed from the national colours. Of course, these had only been recently confirmed, whereas Pearson's selection derived from both the British and French mother countries. It also helped that the blue detracted from the charge that the Pearson Pennant was a partisan Liberal banner.

The boldest part of Pearson's proposal was his intention to push his flag through Parliament as a confidence measure. It was brash, given the nature of the issue alone. It was more so considering the reality that his government did not command a majority in the Commons. He was soon forced to drop the idea.

On the other side of the Commons, John Diefenbaker's Conservatives engaged in ferocious opposition from the outset. The former prime minister had been a lifelong booster of the Canadian Red Ensign. He did indicate that he was open to simplifying it by replacing the shield with a single white fleur-de-lis. However, two-nations designs no longer had a strong following at either end of the linguistic divide.[62] In the meantime, the Tories dug into a filibuster that kept Parliament sitting all summer without resolution.

In September, Pearson finally agreed to submit the question to a parliamentary committee. As in 1945–1946, this led to a flood of submissions that would eventually crest at nearly six thousand. Being the 1960s, they included both the absurdly abstract and the clearly comical. Still, on balance, the proposals displayed the same range and frequency of symbols as in the debate of two decades earlier.

Objective polling on the matter was scarce, but it is safe to say that the debate broke down into two broad camps: the traditionalists and the nationalists. To be clear, each side proclaimed its dedication both to time-honoured symbols and to patriotic values. But their emphases differed markedly.

The traditionalist camp was dominated by backers of the Canadian Red Ensign. It had had a following, generally a growing one, for almost a hundred years. Sentiment was strongest among war veterans, who viewed it as the flag they had fought under. But there was still a minority who favoured the Union Jack, especially among those who most keenly valued the British connection. They included recent immigrants from the United Kingdom and people who lived in areas of the country culturally closer to Britain, such as Newfoundland and Vancouver Island.

The nationalist camp was clearly larger, but it was also more diffuse and less intense in its views. That said, it seems there were two flags in that group that had significant followings. One was the Pearson Pennant. The other was based on a suggestion by historian George Stanley, dean of arts at the Royal Military College (see Figure 49). Stanley proposed using that institution's flag, retaining the red bars on each side, but replacing the Royal Military College emblem in the white centre with a single red maple leaf.[63]

We do not know which of these new alternatives had more support. Nevertheless, there is ample reason to believe that the prime minister's proposal was ahead. That was certainly true in the case of the parliamentary committee examining the various designs.

Once the Canadian Red Ensign had been voted down, the Conservative members of the committee preferred the blue-bar design. However, they secretly voted for the red-bar design to prevent a consensus around the prime minister's flag. The Liberals naturally followed Pearson's preference, but they privately decided that it would be seen as too partisan. They also voted for the Stanley-inspired option.

Politics being politics, while everybody preferred the blue-bars pennant, the red-bars alternative passed unanimously. The matter then returned to the Commons. There, Diefenbaker's forces regrouped for another filibuster, demanding the matter go to referendum. With the debate becoming increasingly polarized, the Tories' Quebec caucus broke with their leader in December and agreed to have the matter voted on through closure.

The rest, as they say, is history. The national flag—to be clear, the first official national flag of Canada—became law on February 15, 1965.

The Flag Debate Since 1965

The reader will notice that the flag of Canada, the "Maple Leaf" or "*Unifolié*," which became official in 1965 (see Figure 50) was not identical to what had come out of the parliamentary committee in 1964.[64] The central emblem had been made fuller, and its points further reduced from thirteen to eleven. This variation, an adjustment allowed within heraldic description, occurred because government experts became convinced that the simpler and stronger the symbol, the better it could be identified at a distance.[65]

It is sometimes alleged that this new leaf was a departure from the more traditional and more natural designs that had appeared on various government insignia, particularly the coat of arms. There is truth in that, but the coat of arms symbol is not very natural to begin with. After all, maple leaves do not actually grow in threes.

Probably the most underappreciated part of the design of the Maple Leaf is the arrangement of the "pales," or the vertical bars. Traditionally, flags of three vertical bars would be divided equally into thirds. There are many such banners in the world, including the national flag of Peru, which also has a red-white-red pattern and was adopted in 1824.

By contrast, the bars on Canada's flag are one-quarter, one-half, and one-quarter of the width respectively, making the middle bar a perfect square. This pattern, grafted into Stanley's original submission by Pearson's point man, member of Parliament John Matheson, was quite innovative.[66] It allowed the dominant symbol to be large while still giving the design

NEW FRANCE
Areas historically claimed by France
TERRE-NEUVE
CANADA
Québec
ACADIE
Île Sainte-Croix
Montréal
Fort Carillon
Rivière Rouge
Fort Détroit
Fort Saint-Louis
LOUISIANE
Fort Caroline
Mobile
Baton-Rouge
La Nouvelle-Orléans

FIGURE 1

FIGURE 2

FIGURE 3

FIGURE 4

FIGURE 5

FIGURE 6

FIGURE 7

FIGURE 8

FIGURE 9

FIGURE 10

FIGURE 11

FIGURE 12

FIGURE 13

FIGURE 14

FIGURE 15

BRITISH
NORTH AMERICA
Original jurisdictions
(New France regions)
British colony
British territory
NORTH-WESTERN TERRITORY
(–)
RUPERT'S LAND
(NORD CANADIEN)
NEWFOUNDLAND
(TERRE-NEUVE)
QUEBEC
(CANADA)
NOVA SCOTIA
(ACADIE)

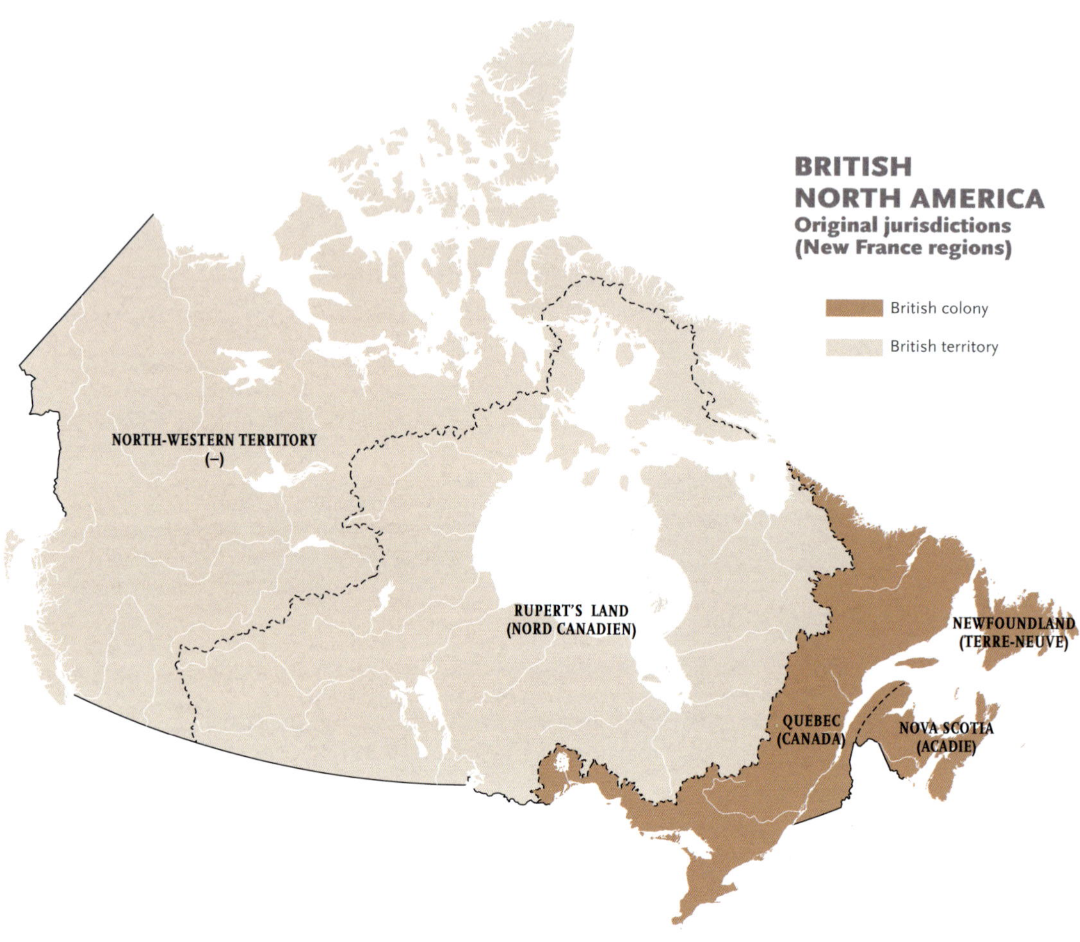

FIGURE 16

FIGURE 17

FIGURE 18

FIGURE 19

FIGURE 20

FIGURE 21

FIGURE 22

FIGURE 23

FIGURE 24

FIGURE 25

FIGURE 26

FIGURE 27

FIGURE 28

FIGURE 29

FIGURE 30

FIGURE 31

FIGURE 32

FIGURE 33

CANADA
Early admissions
to Confederation
Province
(date of admission)
Territory
(date of admission)
British colony
NORTHWEST TERRITORIES
(1870)
BRITISH
COLUMBIA
(1871)
MANITOBA
(1870)
ONTARIO
(1867)
QUEBEC
(1867)
NEWFOUNDLAND
P.E.I.
(1873)
NEW
BRUNSWICK
(1867)
NOVA
SCOTIA
(1867)

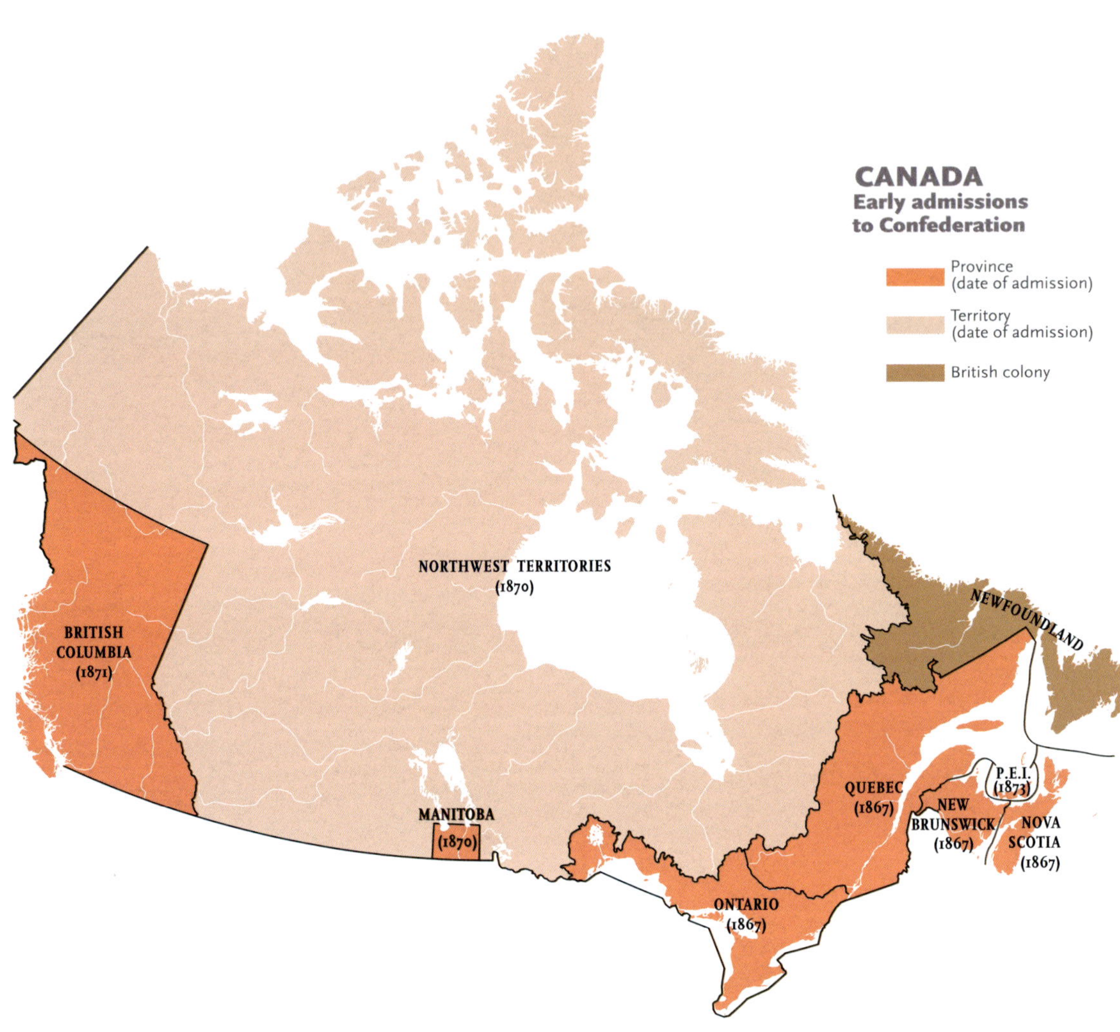

FIGURE 34

FIGURE 35

FIGURE 36

FIGURE 37

FIGURE 38

FIGURE 39

FIGURE 40

FIGURE 41

FIGURE 42

FIGURE 43

FIGURE 44

FIGURE 45

FIGURE 46

FIGURE 47

FIGURE 48

FIGURE 49

FIGURE 50

FIGURE 51

a well-proportioned look. This was christened the "Canadian pale" in blazon,[67] and it has become a feature of many subsequent flags.

A significant minority of the population opposed the new flag in 1965. Its numbers went beyond the traditionalists who favoured the Canadian Red Ensign or the Union Jack. They also included some who genuinely objected to the design, believing it had the feel of a commercial logo.[68]

I would suggest that the opposition reflected an older conception of a flag. The earliest flags were based on or included coats of arms. Their designs were purposely elaborate. Many still are. For instance, the standards of heads of state are usually far more detailed than the banners of their nations.

As flags came to represent broad communities rather than high offices, cleaner patterns became preferred. Many older flags—the Canadian Red Ensign is a perfect example—are now viewed as excessively intricate. Newer model flags risk the opposite: appearing overly simplistic, faddish, or superficial in meaning.

As for the Maple Leaf, I would argue that the "logo" allegation is best judged in context. My own perception, witnessing the flag of Canada flying at international institutions and world events, is that it holds up very well against the range of national flags. Its pattern is strong, unique, and rooted in history.

The number of its opponents diminished rapidly in the years following the Maple Leaf's adoption. Still, there are small numbers of citizens who continue to fly the Canadian Red Ensign, mostly out of dedication to history and tradition. Interestingly, individuals tend to fly the red-leaves version of

1957, whereas groups, particularly veterans' groups, will invariably employ the green-leaves one of 1921.

The more regrettable part of the story was the Pearson government's decision to retain no official role for the Canadian Red Ensign. Contrary to the wishes of most of the opposition, the Royal Union Flag, or Union Jack, was designated in law as a secondary flag. It would continue to be used when appropriate to express Canada's enduring ties to the Crown and the Commonwealth.

Why was this objectionable? To put it simply, having so strongly argued that the Canadian Red Ensign was insufficiently "Canadian," it was truly disingenuous to assert that the national flag of Britain could in some way represent Canada. The alternatives were obvious. Canada's loyalty to the Crown would be better represented by a generic Canadian Royal Standard.[69] And the flag to represent its place in the Commonwealth would indeed have been the Canadian Red Ensign.

That would have been an honourable compromise on Lester Pearson's part. Was he truly beholden to Newfoundland and Labrador Premier Joey Smallwood on the matter, as his supporters claim? Or did he simply refuse to give a small victory to his nemesis, John Diefenbaker? Was he implying that the monarchy was in no way a Canadian institution? Was he worried that the Canadian Red Ensign could become a rallying point for English-Canadian identity at a time when the government was focused on Quebec nationalism?

It is impossible to know the answers to these questions. What we do know is that the decision to sideline the Canadian Red Ensign entirely, despite its considerable following, led to a campaign for its adoption in the provinces, particularly Ontario and Manitoba.[70] In any event, the Commonwealth would eventually adopt its own flag, even if it is almost never flown in Canada.

Of all the lingering questions, the most intriguing is this: Was one of the key premises behind the Maple Leaf, in fact, correct? Was a purely Canadian national flag necessary to fight Quebec sovereignty? Was it, to use the words of John Matheson, urgently needed to "save Canada" from the separatists? The answer is far from self-evident.

As late as the provincial election of 1962, a significant separatist party did not even exist in Quebec. As for the development of the new national flag, French-Canadians—and, for that matter, "ethnic" Canadians—played little role. The small group around Lester Pearson that drove the project forward were all Canadians of British Isles background, notwithstanding their claims to speak for the non-British elements of the population.[71]

The flag debate itself betrayed a general disinterest of Francophone Quebecers in the matter. True, few Francophones had much appetite for the Canadian Red Ensign, either, but the various alternatives elicited little enthusiasm among the *Québécois*. Pearson's successor as prime minister, Pierre Trudeau, bluntly said so at the time.

Subsequent events did little to correct that impression. The truth is that the Quebec sovereignty movement rose dramatically after the *Unifolié* was adopted. From the first separatist parties of 1966 to the first separatist members elected in 1970, to the first separatist government in 1976, to the first referendum in 1980, support for Quebec sovereignty only went up, no matter how often the Maple Leaf was waved.

On the other hand, the tide did eventually turn. As separatist support surged behind the *Fleurdelisé*, could the opponents of Quebec sovereignty have been able to rally behind a British-themed flag? Or under no flag at all? That seems unlikely. But perhaps, in the end, flags really had little to do with any of it.

One more question is worth asking: Is the flag debate truly settled? Is there any possibility of the flag being changed in the future? It is worth exploring, because flag preferences have a way of evolving, if rarely over a few years, then sometimes over the decades, and frequently over the centuries.

Since 1965, no brand new national flag has gained a following, but new variants on the Maple Leaf have arisen. Most are speciality items, designed to appeal to specific groups—the Indigenous and marijuana versions of Canada's flag come to mind. But there is one alternative that warrants some commentary. It is the Canadian Duality Flag (see Figure 51).

The Canadian Duality Flag arose at federalist rallies in the Quebec referendum of 1995 and has been occasionally seen since, especially in the Montreal area. The idea is to replace one-quarter of the red bars on the flag of Canada with blue bars to represent the proportion of Francophones in Canada. The look harkens back to the Pearson Pennant.

While not unattractive, the proposal demonstrates a lack of historical understanding. After all, the hues of the national flag are derived from the historical colours of British-Canadians and French-Canadians—red and white, respectively. Blue may be the colour of Quebec, but it is not the traditional colour of Francophones generally.

There is, of course, no likelihood of the Canadian Duality Flag replacing the current national flag. At present, there is even less chance of any other alternative doing so. It seems that the flag of Canada is as likely to endure as the country itself.

Acknowledgements

WHILE VEXILLOLOGY – Canadian flags in particular – has long been an interest of mine, this project was conceived during the early days of the Covid-19 lockdown. I was fortunate to receive much help along the way.

Thanks first and foremost to Greg Stoicoiu, who meticulously created the illustrations that make this a visually interesting work.

Special thanks to Robb Watt, the former Chief Herald of Canada, for reviewing this work in detail and offering many useful suggestions and amendments.

Thanks to those who provided some of the articles I need during my research, as well as their unique perspectives: Dr. Alistair B. Fraser, Dr. Chris Champion, the late Kevin Harrington of the Canadian Flag Association, and Stephen Murray of the Royal Heraldry Society of Canada.

Thanks to the great team behind publishing this work: John Geiger and all the folks at the Royal Canadian Geographical Society, Ken Whyte and his team at Sutherland House Books, and my irreplaceable agent, Michael Levine and Westwood Creative Artists.

Finally, allow me to acknowledge my brother, Grant, who has provided some useful input on this and many of the other things I have done in life. And I cannot forget my late father, Joseph H. Harper, a published vexillologist in his own right and the person who encouraged my interest in this field from an early age.

I hope I have not missed anyone, but those oversights and any other errors are mine alone.

Stephen J. Harper

Bibliography

Ansoff, Peter, "Sir Charles Fawcett Redux: The Historical Connection Between the East India Company Flag and the Continental Colors," *Proceedings of the 24th International Congress of Vexillology*, 2011, pp. 6–26.

——, "The Flag on Prospect Hill: A Response to Byron DeLear," *Raven*, Vol. 22, 2015, pp. 1–26.

Arbuckle, Graeme, *Customs and Traditions of the Canadian Navy*, 1984.

Archambault, R. P., *Le Drapeau canadien-français*, 1928.

Archbold, Rick, *A Flag for Canada*, 2008.

Baillargé, Frédéric Alexandre, *Le drapeau canadien-français: nos raisons*, 1904.

Band, Charles P., and Stovel, Emilie L., *Our Flag and Coat of Arms: A Concise Illustrated History of our Flag and the Coats of Arms of the Dominion of Canada and Its Various Provinces*, second edition, 1919.

Barraclough, E. M. C., and Crampton, W. G., *Flags of the World*, second edition, 1981.

Beaudoin, François, "Flags of Quebec," *Flag Bulletin*, Vol. 23–5, No. 107, September–October 1984, pp. 149–163.

Biron, Luc-André, *Le Drapeau canadien*, second edition, 1964.

Bizier, Hélène-Andrée, and Paulette, Claude, *Fleur de lys: D'hier à aujourd'hui*, 1997.

Blondel, Edouard, "Les drapeaux canadiens," *La Presse*, April 10, 1920, pp. 1 & 8.

Bone, James, "Donald Nelson Baird and the 1945–46 Parliamentary Flag Design Committee," Library and Archives Canada Blog, 2021, online.

Boulton, D'Arcy Jonathan Dacre, "Towards a More Canadian Regal-Regnal Achievement: An Historical and Semeiotic Analysis of the 1921 Achievement, with Proposals for Modifications of Its Elements," *Alta Studia Heraldica*, 2009, pp. 137–190; 2010, pp. 159–230.

Bouvier, Luc, "Histoire des drapeaux québécois: du tricolore canadien au fleurdelisé québécois," *Heraldry in Canada/L'Héraldique au Canada*, Vol. 28, No. 1, March 1994, pp. 30–41; Vol. 28, No. 2, June 1994, pp. 22–33; Vol. 28, No. 3, September 1994, pp. 25–32; Vol. 28, No. 4, December 1994, pp. 25–33; Vol. 29, No. 1, March 1995, pp. 25–33; Vol. 29, No. 2, June 1995, pp. 27–33.

Boyes, Aaron W., *Towards the "Federated States of North America:" the Advocacy for Political Union between Canada and the United States 1885–1896*, 2016.

Brady, Hugh L., "Dominion Day Exercises: Early Efforts to Develop a Canadian Identity," *NAVA News*, Vol. 46–3, No. 219, July–September 2013, pp. 1 & 3–5.

——, "'But It was Ours:' The Red Ensign, Dominion Day, and the Effects of Patriotic Memory on the Canadian Flag Debate," *Raven*, Vol. 23, 2016, pp. 19–54.

Braverman, Doreen, *Flags tell the Story of Canada*, 1995.

Bucchioni, Josh, "Hoist Up the Flag: The British Red Ensign," Colonial Williamsburg, 2020, online.

Campbell, Colin, "The Flag of our Country," *Canadian Almanac*, 1894, pp. 195–204.

——, "The Imperial and Canadian Flags," *Canadian Almanac*, 1895, pp. 214–17.

Campbell, Gordon, and Evans, I. O., *The Book of Flags*, seventh edition, 1974.

Carr, H. Gresham, *Flags of the World*, revised edition, 1961.

Chadwick, E. M., "The Canadian Flag," *Canadian Almanac*, 1896, pp. 227–228 & 233.

Champagne, Antoine, *Nouvelles études sur les La-Vérendrye et le poste de L'Ouest*, 1971.

Champion, Chris P., "A Very British Coup: Canadianism, Quebec, and Ethnicity in the Flag Debate 1964–1965," *Journal of Canadian Studies/Revue d'études canadiennes*, Vol. 40, No. 3, September 2006, pp. 68–99.

Charrié, Pierre, *Drapeaux et étendards du Roi*, 1989.

Chartrand, René, "Les drapeaux en Nouvelle-France," *Conservation Canada*, Vol. 1, No. 1, 1974, pp. 24–26.

——, "The Flags of New France," *Flag Bulletin*, Vol. 15–1, No. 59, January–February 1976, pp. 13–21.

——, "Les drapeaux militaires en Nouvelle-France," *Revue d'histoire de la culture matérielle*, No. 42–1, Automne 1995, pp. 39–46.

Chauveau, Pierre-Joseph-Olivier, *Discours: prononcé à la cérémonie de la pose de la pierre angulaire du monument dédié par souscription nationale à la mémoire des braves tombés sur la plaine d'Abraham le 28 avril 1760*, 1855.

——, "Prononcé sur la tombe de M. F.-X. Garneau," *Histoire du Canada: depuis sa découverte jusqu'à nos jours*, Vol. 4, fourth edition, 1882, pp. 267–276.

Comité de Québec, *Le drapeau national des canadiens-français: un choix légitime et populaire*, 1904.

Costaine, Thomas B., *The White and the Gold: The French Regime in Canada*, 1954.

Crampton, William, *The Observer's Book of Flags*, 1979.

Crémazie, Octave, *Le drapeau de Carillon*, 1858.

Croft, James, "Civic Flags of the Northwest Territories," *Flag Bulletin*, Vol. 28–1/2/3/4, No. 130, January–August 1989, pp. 44–78.

Cumberland, Barlow, *History of the Union Jack and Flags of the Empire: Their Origin, Proportions and Meanings as Tracing the Constitutional Development of the British Realm, and with Reference to Other National Ensigns*, third edition, 1909.

Davidson, J. A., "Standing on Guard for Thee: Maple Leaves, Union Jacks, and a Dauntless Hero," *The Beaver*, Vol. 70, No. 3, June–July 1990, pp. 14–20.

Davies, T. R., "Some Notes on the Vexillum and the Cross of St. George," *Flag Bulletin*, Vol. 16–3, No. 66, May–June 1977, pp. 84–88.

DeLear, Byron, "Revisiting the Flag at Prospect Hill: Grand Union or Just British?", *Raven*, Vol. 21, 2014, pp. 19–70.

Denison, George T., *The Struggle for Imperial Unity: Recollections and Experiences*, 1909.

Desbarats, George, "The Provincial Arms and the Dominion Flags," *Canadian Illustrated News*, May 6, 1871, p. 281.

Desjardins, Gustave, *Recherches sur les drapeaux français: oriflamme, bannière de France, marques nationales, couleurs du roi, drapeau de l'armée, pavillons de la marine*, 1874.

Diceman, Harold, "Modern Canadian Military Flags," *Flag Bulletin*, Vol. 19–3/4/5, No. 84, May–October 1980, pp. 127–138.

Diefenbaker, John G., *One Canada: The Tumultuous Years 1962–1967*, 1977.

Doughty, Arthur G., "Le drapeau de la Nouvelle-France," *Mémoires et comptes rendus de la Société Royale du Canada*, Ser. 3, Vol. 20, May 1926, pp. 43–46.

Drouin, Mathieu, "Drapeau de l'infanterie française: ce drapeau fleurdelysé aurait été retrouvé sur les lieux emblématique de la bataille des Plaines d'Abraham," *Canada's History/Histoire Canada*, 12 décembre 2022, online.

Dunbar, Francis J., and Harper, Joseph H., *Old Colours Never Die: A Record of Colours and Military Flags in Canada*, second edition, 2013.

Etchells, Arthur, "French Naval Flags Under the *Ancien Régime*," *Vexillum*, No. 25, March 2024, pp. 14–15.

Evans, I. O., *Flags of the World*, 1970.

——, "The British Ensigns," *Flag Bulletin*, Vol. 21–5, No. 96, September–October 1982, pp. 165–170.

Ewart, John Skirving, "The Canadian Flag," *Canadian Magazine*, Vol. 30, No. 1, 1907, pp. 332–335.

——, *Sir John A. Macdonald and the Canadian Flag*, 1907.

Filiatrault, Elphège, *Aux Canadiens-français: notre drapeau*, 1903.

——, *Carillon! Carillon! Le drapeau national des Canadiens-français*, 1904.

——, *Nos couleurs nationales*, 1905.

Fleming, Sandford, "The Canadian Flag: Proposal for the Meteor Flag of the Dominion," *The Week*, May 31, 1895, cover & p. 639.

Fraser, Alistair B., "A Canadian Flag for Canada," *Raven*, Vol. 1, 1994, pp. 30–40.

——, *The Flags of Canada*, 1998.

Fraser, Blair, *The Search for Identity: Canada 1945–1967*, 1967.

Gaffen, Fred, "British Flags Presented to the Indians," *Flag Bulletin*, Vol. 21–5, No. 96, September–October 1982, pp. 153–164.

Gigandet, Hank, "Canadian Duality Flag Proposal," *NAVA News*, Vol. 37–1, No. 181, January–March 2004, p. 3.

Good, Jonathan, "Colonial Seals of Canada," *Heraldry in Canada/L'Héraldique au Canada*, Vol. 55, No. 3–4, December 2021, pp. 44–53.

Gordon, W. J., *Flags of the World: Their Story and Associations*, 1915.

Government of Canada, *The National Flag of Canada*, 1966.

——, "Posters of Historic Flags," Canada.ca, 2007, online.

——, "1963–1965: The Birth of Canada's National Flag," Canada.ca, 2023, online.

Government of Nova Scotia, "New Flag of the Office of the Lieutenant Governor of Nova Scotia," *Royal Gazette*, Vol. 233, No. 21, May 22, 2024, pp. 750–751.

Governor General of Canada, "The Public Register of Arms, Flags, and Badges of Canada," gg.ca, 2023, online.

Greaves, Kevin, *A Canadian Heraldic Primer*, 2000.

Grebstad, David W., *The Flag of Our Fathers? The Manitoba Provincial Flag and British Cultural hegemony in Manitoba 1870–1966*, *Raven*, Vol. 23, 2016, pp. 55–79.

Groulx, Lionel, *Le drapeau canadien-français*, 1944.

Harrington, Kevin, "Indian, Inuit, and Metis Flags of Canada," *Flag Bulletin*, Vol. 28–1/2/3/4, No. 130, January–August 1989, pp. 146–167.

——, "The Flags of Francophonie in Canada," *Flag Bulletin*, Vol. 31–4, No. 147, July–August 1992, pp. 139–152.

——, "The Name, Colours and Symbols of Quebec," *NAVA News*, Vol. 31–1, No. 154, January–February 1998, pp. 1–3.

Hudson's Bay Company, "The Flags of the HBC," HBC Heritage, 2021, online.

Hulme, F. Edward, *Flags of the World: Their History, Blazonry and Associations*, 1893.

Joy, John, "On the Union Flag," *Flag Bulletin*, Vol. 12–2, No. 44, Summer 1973, pp. 44–54.

Kannik, Preben, *The Flag Book*, third edition, 1959.

Kaye, Ted, "New Mexico Tops State/Provincial Flags Survey: Georgia Loses by Wide Margin," *NAVA News*, Vol. 34–2, No. 170, April–June 2001, pp. 4–5.

——, *"Good" Flag, "Bad" Flag*, 2006.

Knox, John, *The Siege of Quebec: And the Campaigns in North America 1757–1760*, 1769.

Koch, Phil, "Setting the Standards of New France," *The Beaver*, Vol. 88, No. 1, February–March 2008, p. 12.

Ligue du drapeau national, *Pour un drapeau national/For a National Flag*, 1943.

Liston, James T., "The Union Flag: Legal Status and Popular Perception," *Flag Bulletin*, Vol. 36–6, No. 178, November–December 1997, pp. 246–262.

Loynes, Louis, "British Flag Proportions," *Flag Bulletin*, Vol. 12–2, No. 44, Summer 1973, pp. 84–85.

Lux-Wurm, P. C., "The Development and Meanings of White as a French National Color," *Flag Bulletin*, Vol. 12–4, No. 46, Winter 1973, pp. 129–135.

MacLeod, D. Peter, and Boucher, C. Michel. "The Drapeau de Carillon: History and Legend," *Flag Bulletin*, Vol. 32–2, No. 151, March–April 1993, pp. 66–87.

Magnan, Charles-Joseph, *Le Carillon-Sacré-Cœur: Le drapeau national des Canadiens français*, 1939.

Magnan, Hormisdas, "Les drapeaux arborés dans la province de Québec," *Bulletin des recherches historiques: bulletin d'archéologie, des recherches historiques*, Vol. 25, No. 5, May 1919, pp. 129–149.

——, *Cinquantenaire de notre hymne nationale "O Canada, terre de nos aïeux: les origines de nos drapeaux et chants nationaux armoiries, emblèmes, devises,"* 1929.

Maple Leaf Mills, *Flags of Empire*, 1941.

Martucci, David B., "Flag and Symbol Usage in Early New England," *Raven*, Vol. 13, 2006, pp. 1–40.

Matheson, John Ross, "Canada's Flag: Introduction," *Flag Bulletin*, Vol. 17–3, No. 72, May–June 1978, pp. 84–92.

——, "Canada's Flag: Canada Obtains Arms (Part I)," *Flag Bulletin*, Vol. 17–6, No. 75, November–December 1978, pp. 172–192.

——, "Canada's Flag: Canada Obtains Arms (Part II)," *Flag Bulletin*, Vol. 18–3, No. 78, May–June 1979, pp. 89–101.

——, *Canada's Flag: A Search for a Country*, second edition, 1986.

Maury, Arthur, *Les emblèmes et les drapeaux de la France: Le coq gaulois*, 1904.

McCandless, Byron, and Grosvenor, Gilbert, *Flags of the World*, 1917.

Mioque, Nicolas, "Les pavillons de la marine sous l'Ancien Régime," Trois-Ponts, 2015, online.

Montreal Star, "The Seized Buttons: In Spite of the Government's Vigilance Some Are in Circulation–Some Brass, Some Celluloid–Brass Ones found in the House of a Gentleman Holding a Government Position," *Montreal Star*, July 21, 1900, p. 13.

Newman, Peter C., *The Distemper of our Times: Canadian Politics in Transition*, 1968.

Nicholls, Bruce, "A Sense of Proportion," *Flag Bulletin*, Vol. 26–1/2/3, No. 120, January–June 1987, pp. 138–142.

Nicholson, Katie, "From Snakes to Spartans: The Meaning Behind Some of the

Flags Convoy Protesters are Carrying," Canadian Broadcasting Corporation, February 16, 2022, online.

O'Neill, Paul, "The Story of Newfoundland's Native Flag," *Flag Bulletin*, Vol. 15–6, No. 63, November–December 1976, pp. 184–198.

Pasch, Georges, "Flags of the Americas, 1500–1667," *Flag Bulletin*, Vol. 18–5, No. 80, October–November 1979, pp. 141–184.

——, "French Attitudes towards the Symbols of France," *Flag Bulletin*, Vol. 20–4, No. 89, July–August 1981, pp. 119–140.

Pass, Forrest D., "'A Red Rag to an Infuriated Bull:' American Flags, Canadian Vexilloclasts, and the Origins of Canadian Flag Culture 1880–1930," *Raven*, Vol. 23, 2016, pp. 81–105.

——, "Les drapeaux oubliés," Le blogue de Bibliothèque et Archives Canada, 2020, online.

——, "Five Myths about the Arms of Canada," Library and Archives Canada Blog, 2021, online.

Patterson, Bruce, "The Red Ensign and the Maple Leaf: Canada's Two Flag Traditions," *Raven*, Vol. 23, 2016, pp. 1–17.

Perrin, W. G., *British Flags: Their Early History, and Their Development at Sea, with an Account of the Origin of the Flag as a National Device*, 1922.

Philippe, Lucien, "The French Tricolor and its Influence on Flags throughout the World," *Flag Bulletin*, Vol. 10–2/3, No. 37, Spring–Summer 1971, pp. 55–68.

Pinoteau, Hervé, *La symbolique royale française: Ve-XVIIIe siècles*, 2003.

Pope, Joseph, *The Flag of Canada*, eighth edition, 1912.

Rabbow, Arnold, "A New Constellation: What Did the First Stars and Stripes Look Like?" *Flag Bulletin*, Vol. 19–2, No. 83, March–April 1980, pp. 47–64.

Racette, Calvin, *Flags of the Métis*, 1987.

Raeside, Rob, "National and Provincial/Territorial Symbols in Municipal Flags in Canada: Patriotism at the Community Level?", *Vexillum*, No. 12, December 2020, pp. 16–23.

Reynolds, Kenneth W., "'To Make the Unmistakable Signal 'Canada:' The Canadian Army's 'Battle Flag' during the Second World War," *Raven*, Vol. 14, 2007, pp. 1–33.

——, "A Glimpse into Vexillology by the Canadian Armed Forces Past and Present," *Flag Research Quarterly*, No. 2, June 2013, pp. 14–16.

——, "'A Symbol of our Place in the World:' The Raising of the National Flag on Canadian Warships, 15 February 1965," *Flag Research Quarterly*, No. 8, February 2016, pp. 1 & 3–15.

Richard, Bernard, *Petite histoire du drapeau français*, 2017.

Rogers, David, "A Flag for the Empire," *Flag Bulletin*, Vol. 17–5, No. 74, September–October 1978, pp. 158–160.

Rothery, Guy, *ABC of Heraldry*, 1915.

Russell, E. C., *Customs and Traditions of the Canadian Armed Forces*, 1980.

Smith, Whitney, "New Flags: Canada," *Flag Bulletin*, Vol. 2–2, No. 6, Winter 1963, p. 19.

——, "New Flags: Canada," *Flag Bulletin*, Vol. 3–4, No. 12, Summer 1964, pp. 47–48.

——, "The History of Canadian Flags," *Flag Bulletin*, Vol. 4–3, No. 15, Spring 1965, pp. 38 & 56–59.

——, "Canadian Provincial Flags," *Flag Bulletin*, Vol. 4–3, No. 15, Spring 1965, pp. 39–47.

——, "Canadian Flag Miscellany," *Flag Bulletin*, Vol. 4–3, No. 15, Spring 1965, pp. 50–51.

——, "Political and Military Flags of Canada," *Flag Bulletin*, Vol. 4–3, No. 15, Spring 1965, pp. 52–55.

——, "New Flags: Ontario," *Flag Bulletin*, Vol. 4–4, No. 16, Summer 1965, p. 61.

——, "New Flags: Manitoba," *Flag Bulletin*, Vol. 5–3, No. 19, Spring 1966, pp. 88–90.

——, *The Flag Book of the United States*, 1970.

——, "The Scots Union Flag," *Flag Bulletin*, Vol. 12–2, No. 44, Summer 1973, pp. 55–58.

——, *Flags Through the Ages and Across the World*, 1975.

——, "An Introduction to Canada's Flag," *Flag Bulletin*, Vol. 17–3, No. 72, May–June 1978, p. 83.

——, "Carillon," *Flag Bulletin*, Vol. 32–4, No. 153, July–August 1993, pp. 180–182.

——, "Flags in the News: United Kingdom of Great Britain," *Flag Bulletin*, Vol. 39–2, No. 192, March–April 2000, pp. 50–60.

Spence, D. Ralph, "An Outline History of Canada's Flags," *Flag Bulletin*, Vol. 19–3/4/5, No. 84, May–October 1980, pp. 319–327.

Stanley, George F. G., "Flag Memorandum," web.archive.org, March 23, 1964, online.

——, *The Story of Canada's Flag: A Historical Sketch*, 1965.

Stevenson, Christophe, "100e anniversaire des armoiries du Canada–Factum Armis–100th Anniversary of the Royal Arms of Canada," *Heraldry in Canada/L'Héraldique au Canada*, Vol. 56, No. 1–4, December 2022, pp. 5–80.

Stursberg, Peter, *Lester Pearson and the Dream of Unity*, second edition, 1978.

Styring, John S., "House Flags: Part I," *Flag Bulletin*, Vol. 2–2, No. 6, Winter 1963, pp. 15–16.

Sulte, Benjamin, *Histoire des Canadiens-français 1608–1880: origine, histoire, religion, guerres, découvertes, colonisation, coutumes, vie domestique, sociale et politique, développement, avenir, 1882–1884.*

——, "Le pavillon canadien," *Bulletin de la Société normande de géographie*, September–October 1895, pp. 309–311.

——, "Le drapeau tricolore au Canada," *Bulletin des Recherches historiques*, Vol. 3, No. 2, February 1897, pp. 29–30.

——, "Le drapeau tricolore en Canada," *Bulletin des Recherches historiques*, Vol. 10, No. 5, May 1904, pp. 151–157.

——, "Couleurs Nationals," *Mélanges historiques: études éparses et inédites de Benjamin Sulte*, Vol. 15, 1929, pp. 66–68.

Swan, Conrad, *Canada: Symbols of Sovereignty*, 1977.

Szala, John R. B., "Joan of Arc's Standard," *Flag Bulletin*, Vol. 11–4, No. 42, Winter 1972, pp. 418–424.

——, "All You Ever Wanted to Know about 'Oriflamme,'" *NAVA News*, Vol. 16–1, No. 64, January–February 1983, p. 1.

——, "Acadian Flag Is 100 Years Old," *NAVA News*, Vol. 17–5, No. 74, September–October 1984, p. 1.

Tallon, Beverley, "HBC Flag: Tales and Treasures from the Rich Legacy of the Hudson's Bay Company," *Canada's History/Histoire Canada*, March 8, 2011, online.

Vachon, Auguste, "Le Red Ensign au Canada: De Pierre Le Moyne d'Iberville à John George Diefenbaker," *Heraldry in Canada/L'Héraldique au Canada*, Vol. 14, No. 3, September 1980, pp. 2–10.

——, "Les drapeaux oubliés," *Heraldry in Canada/L'Héraldique au Canada,* Vol. 15, No. 2, June 1981, pp. 12–23.

——, "Flags of Canada: An Historical Overview," *Flag Bulletin*, Vol. 27–3, No. 126, May–June 1988, pp. 88–102.

——, "La fleur de lis seule: marque d'autorité et de possession royales en Nouvelle-France," *Heraldic Science Héraldique,* 1990, online.

——, "Bannière de France et Pavillon blanc en Nouvelle-France," *Heraldry in Canada/L'Héraldique au Canada,* Vol. 42, No. 1–4, December 2008, pp. 19–33.

——, "Did Alexander Scott Carter Give Canada Its National Colours?" *Heraldry in Canada/L'Héraldique au Canada*, Vol. 44, No. 1–4, December 2010, pp. 9–18.

——, "Les origines du castor et de la feuille d'érable comme emblèmes canadiens," *Heraldry in Canada/L'Héraldique au Canada*, Vol. 45, No. 3–4, December 2011, pp. 50–69.

——, "The Armorial Bearings of Nova Scotia: Why Two Official Versions?" *Alta Studia Heraldica*, Vol. 4, 2012, pp. 231–246.

——, "Une opinion sur les armes du Québec," *Heraldic Science Héraldique*, 2013, online.

——, "A Precursor to the Flag of Nova Scotia," *Heraldic Science Héraldique*, 2013, online.

——, "Les pavillons de la marine marchande en Nouvelle-France," *Heraldic Science Héraldique*, 2014, online.

——, "Canada's Coat of Arms: Defining a Country within an Empire," *Heraldic Science Héraldique*, 2014, online.

——, "Variations in the Arms of Sovereignty Connected with Canada: A Pictorial Overview, *Heraldic Science Héraldique*, 2016, online.

——, "La recherche de symboles identitaires canadiens," *Heraldic Science Héraldique*, 2019, online.

Wade, F. C., *The Canadian Flag and Our Schools*, 1908.

Willis, Ronald E., *Historical Flags of Canada*, 1965.

Wise, Terence, *Military Flags of the World 1618–1900*, 1977.

Wright, Glenn T., "First Flags: A Report on Research Undertaken to Identify and Locate Canada's First Maple Leaf Flags," *Flag Bulletin*, Vol. 47–1/2, No. 231, January–April 2008, pp. 3–55.

Wright, W. J., *Our Flag: What It Means, the Royal, Dominion and Provincial Arms, a Sketch*, 1904.

Notes

1 Northlea is the northern part of the neighbourhood of Leaside, which is located northeast of downtown Toronto. From 1913 until 1966, Leaside was a separate, incorporated town. I was born there (1959) and lived in the area until Grade 7 (1971).

2 These alternative colours are all noted in Gustave Desjardins, *Recherches sur les drapeaux français,* 1874, pp. 58–62.

3 Ibid., p. v.

4 Ibid.

5 The transition is discussed at length in Hervé Pinoteau, *La symbolique royale française*, 2003, pp. 450–456.

6 These are outlined in detail in Auguste Vachon, "Bannière de France et Pavillon blanc en Nouvelle-France," *Heraldry in Canada/L'Héraldique au Canada,* December 2008, pp. 19–33.

7 Desjardins, op. cit., pp. 112–113.

8 See "French Ensigns."

9 Desjardins, op. cit., pp. iii–iv.

10 Ibid., pp. iv & 29–36.

11 Ibid., pp. 40–43.

12 See René Chartrand, "Les drapeaux militaires en Nouvelle-France," *Revue d'histoire de la culture matérielle, Automne 1995,* pp. 39–46.

13 René Chartrand, "Les drapeaux en Nouvelle-France," *Conservation Canada*, 1974, pp. 24–25.

14 The royal shield was added in 1661, and the crown and collars were added in 1689. For a commentary on the usage of these various versions of the *Pavillon bleu*, see Auguste Vachon, "Les pavillons de la marine marchande en Nouvelle-France," *Heraldic Science Héraldique*, 2014.

15 One was noted by John Knox, *The Siege of Quebec*, 1769, p. 292, but its three gold fleurs-de-lis were also encircled by gold laurels.

16 The chief dominion archivist and noted Quebec historian, Arthur G. Doughty, argued that various sketches in New France showed gold fleurs-de-lis on a white flag. However, most observers now believe these drawings are too indistinct to draw such precise conclusions. See "Le drapeau de la Nouvelle-France," *Mémoires et comptes rendus de la Société Royale du Canada*, 1926, p. 46.

17 Pinoteau, op. cit., pp. 638–651, discusses the emergence of white as the national colour of royal France over the centuries. Vachon, "Bannière de France et Pavillon blanc en Nouvelle-France," gives examples of its similar status in New France.

18 Vachon, "Bannière de France et Pavillon blanc en Nouvelle-France," gives examples of both state and religious symbols added to the Pavillon blanc in New France.

19 See Chapter 2, "British Colonial Flags."

20 For a detailed description of Joan of Arc's flags, see Desjardins, op. cit., pp. 27–28.

21 Pierre-Joseph-Olivier Chauveau, *Discours*, 1855. p. 4.

22 Katie Nicholson, "From Snakes to Spartans," Canadian Broadcasting Corporation, February 16, 2022.

23 This is described in Hormisdas Magnan, *Cinquantenaire de notre hymne nationale "O Canada, terre de nos aïeux,"* 1929, p. 45.

24 This was believed to be the original colour of the *Drapeau de Carillon*, but that is uncertain. It may have been white or an off-white/cream colour.

25 This event is reviewed in detail in Luc Bouvier, "Histoire des drapeaux québécois," *Heraldry in Canada/L'Héraldique au Canada*, part IV.5, December 1994.

26 The characteristics generally identified with strong and weak flag design are discussed in Ted Kaye, *"Good" Flag, "Bad" Flag*, 2006.

27 The Flag of Quebec has been rated 3rd out of 72 North American subnational flags..

See Ted Kaye, "New Mexico Tops State/Provincial Flags Survey," *NAVA News*, April-June 2001, pp. 4-5.

28 See Chapter 2, "Provincial Legacy Flags."

29 Cabot, however, with the permission of Henry VII, used his sovereign's Royal Standard to plant his claims in the New World. The English Royal Standard was then a quartering of the royal shields of France and England, reflecting an ongoing English claim to the French throne.

30 This supposition has been made in many sources. The earliest I have found it is in W. J. Gordon, *Flags of the World*, 1915, pp. 59–60.

31 See Chapter 1, "The Flag of the Kingdom of France."

32 I have seen no reference to the flags of the Commonwealth appearing in either Newfoundland or Nova Scotia. However, given that their governors at the time had been appointed by Oliver Cromwell, it seems likely that they would have flown there.

33 Any British colony in Canada could have employed a localized Blue Ensign on its vessels from 1865. However, I am not aware whether any did so before the federal government. Sometimes seen is the Vancouver Island Blue Ensign, but it is a modern creation and was not used during its existence as a separate colony (1849–1866). See Alistair B. Fraser, *The Flags of Canada*, Chapter 10, "British Columbia: Municipalities and Regions," 1998.

34 From 1911 to 1965, the Canadian Blue Ensign flew on the front (jack) staff of RCN ships, while the White Ensign flew on the back (stern) staff and, until 1961, on the centre (masthead) staff, when it was replaced by the Canadian Red Ensign. See Graeme Arbuckle, *Customs and Traditions of the Canadian Navy*, 1984, pp. 29–31.

35 See Chapter 3, "The Flag Debate 1918–1945."

36 One example is at the former, now abandoned, HBC regional headquarters of York Factory on Hudson Bay, which I visited in 2012.

37 See Chapter 3, "The Flag Debate 1867–1918."

38 Pink is generally not recognized as a distinctive colour ("tincture") in heraldry. However, because of the unique use of pink on the Newfoundland Tricolour and

its subsequent use on the arms of some Newfoundlanders, the Canadian Heraldic Authority recognizes "rose" as a separate tincture.

39 See Chapter 1, "The Flag of Quebec."

40 The flag of Nova Scotia has been rated twelfth out of seventy-two North American subnational flags. See Ted Kaye, "New Mexico Tops State/Provincial Flags Survey," *NAVA News*, April–June 2001, pp. 4–5.

41 See Chapter 3, "The Flag Debate Since 1965."

42 See Chapter 1, "Other French Legacy Flags."

43 The previously mentioned survey rated the flags of Ontario and Manitoba forty-third and forty-fourth out of seventy-two, the lowest among Canadian provincial/territorial flags. See Kaye, op. cit.

44 Another relevant example is the flag of the Kainai First Nation (the "Blood Tribe") of southern Alberta, which adds local symbolism to a sky-blue British ensign, all of which is placed on a white background. I am an honorary chief of that First Nation.

45 A prominent example of this thinking was the view of Thomas Mulvey, Canada's under-secretary of state. He explained why the committee that established Canada's arms in 1921, of which he was a member, omitted the beaver: "It was decided that as a member of the Rat Family, a Beaver was not appropriate.... The Canadian Merchant Marine [*sic* for the Beaver Line] displayed a Beaver on their House-Flag and they have ever since been colloquially known as 'The Rat Line.'" See Alistair B. Fraser, *The Flags of Canada*, Chapter 1, "Canada's National Symbols: The Beaver," 1998.

46 The best analysis of this issue is Auguste Vachon, "Les origines du castor et de la feuille d'érable comme emblèmes canadiens," *Heraldry in Canada/L'Héraldique au Canada*, December 2011, pp. 50–69.

47 To be more precise, Canada was created by three British colonies: New Brunswick, Nova Scotia, and the United Province of Canada. The last, sometimes called the "Canadas," was a union of Ontario ("Canada West," previously Upper Canada) and Quebec ("Canada East," previously Lower Canada). That union had proven to be dysfunctional. Confederation both unified the colonies (via the federal government) and separated Ontario and Quebec (as provinces) once again.

48 This map simplifies areas in which disputed jurisdiction was not clarified by British authorities until later, that is, in the case of the Arctic Islands (1880) and Labrador (1927).

49 See Chapter 2, "British Colonial Flags."

50 See Chapter 2, "British Ensigns."

51 George Stanley, *The Story of Canada's Flag*, 1965, pp. 26–27.

52 Ibid., p. 28.

53 See Chapter 1, "The Flag of Quebec."

54 The "Independence of Canada" flag was likely the product of an individual or group promoting full Canadian sovereignty. An article about the button appeared around this time. It hints at American origins but admits that its creators were unknown. See "The Seized Buttons," *Montreal Star*, July 21, 1900, p. 13. Such independence movements did exist in Canada during that era, along with groups favouring Imperial federation and North American union. However, far more Canadians preferred to simply remain autonomous within the British Empire. For an account of an 1892 debate between these four groups, see Aaron W. Boyes, *Towards the "Federated States of North America,"* p. 159.

55 This was done decades ago for most provinces, but the new pattern was not adopted by Nova Scotia until 2024.

56 To be clear, prime ministers, who are heads of government and not heads of state, do not possess their own flags. The protocol is that they employ the national flag. However, in the spring of 1945, when Mackenzie King visited San Francisco for the drafting of the United Nations Charter, he used this variant of the Union Jack, made of silk, in a design that would be more fitting for a governor general. After that, it appears that he reverted to the more appropriate Canadian Red Ensign. See Fraser, op. cit., Chapter 2, "Heads of State: The Flag of the Prime Minister."

57 Colonel Archer Fortescue "Scotty" Duguid was the director of the Canadian Army's Historical Section from 1921 to 1945. His role in the design of the Canadian Battle Flag around the time of the 1925 committee is documented. See especially Kenneth W. Reynolds, "To Make the Unmistakable Signal 'Canada,'" *Raven*, 2007,

p. 8. Duguid's design would eventually lead to the Pearson Pennant. See "The Flag Debate 1957–1965".

58 See Chapter 1, "The Flag of Quebec."

59 This was done by Order-in-Council on September 5, 1945. See Stanley, op. cit., p. 49.

60 This is, of course, my opinion. To me, the leaf looks halfway between a maple leaf and an oak leaf. The original design, submitted by Donald Nelson Baird of Truro, Nova Scotia, had a maple leaf much closer to the one on today's national flag, although it still has a more "natural" look. See James Bone, "Donald Nelson Baird and the 1945–46 Parliamentary Flag Design Committee," Library and Archives Canada Blog, 2021.

61 See Government of Canada, "1963–1965: The Birth of Canada's National Flag," Canada.ca, 2023, online.

62 See "The Flag Debate 1918–1945."

63 See George Stanley, "Flag Memorandum," web.archive.org, 1964, online.

64 Besides developing the Pearson Pennant, Alan Beddoe had provided the original graphic rendering of Stanley's flag concept, while Ken Donovan of the Canadian Government Exhibition Commission and his daughter Joan O'Malley had created the prototypes. See Government of Canada, op. cit.

65 The final design of the flag was the responsibility of Patrick Reid, director of the Canadian Government Exhibition Commission. Among those under him was Jacques St-Cyr, a military veteran who had received expert instruction in graphic art and design at schools in Montreal, New York, and London. St-Cyr created the final shape of the maple leaf. See John Matheson, *Canada's Flag*, second edition, 1986, p. 178.

66 Matheson had taken the idea from George Bist, another military veteran and graphic designer. Bist had created a flag with blue bars and a single red maple leaf on a central white square. This was the design favoured by the New Democratic Party. See ibid., pp. 125–126.

67 The term "Canadian pale" was coined by Dr. Conrad Swan, later Sir Conrad Swan.

He had been the first Canadian ever appointed to the College of Arms in London and rose to be garter principal king of arms. See ibid., p. 134.

68 Another objection to the Maple Leaf flag, at least initially, was how poorly the large red sections fared when exposed to the elements. Before the flag became official, this was rectified by Günter Wyszecki of the National Research Council of Canada, who developed the official shade of red. See Government of Canada, op. cit.

69 Just such a flag—the Canadian coat of arms in rectangular form without a personal mark—is now the Canadian Royal Standard of King Charles III.

70 See Chapter 2, "Provincial Legacy Flags."

71 This is ably exposed in Chris Champion, "A Very British Coup," *Journal of Canadian Studies*, September 2006, 68–99.